LAURA INGALLS WILDER
AND
THE AMERICAN FRONTIER

Five Perspectives

Edited by
Dwight M. Miller

University Press of America,® Inc.
Lanham · New York · Oxford

Copyright © 2002 by
University Press of America,® Inc.
4501 Forbes Boulevard, Suite 200
Lanham, Maryland 20706
UPA Acquisitions Department (301) 459-3366

12 Hid's Copse Rd.
Cumnor Hill, Oxford OX2 9JJ

Library of Congress Cataloging-in-Publication Data

Laura Ingalls Wilder and the American frontier : five perspectives /
edited by Dwight M. Miller.
p.   cm
"Essays in this volume originated as papers for the conference ...
hosted by the Herbert Hoover Presidential Library and Museum
September 25-26, 1988"—Introduction.
Includes index.
1. Wilder, Laura Ingalls, 1867-1957—Criticism and interpretation.
2. Women and literature—United States—History—20th century.
3. Historical fiction, American—History and criticism. 4. Children's
stories, American—History and criticism. 5. Domestic fiction,
American—History and criticism. 6. Frontier and pioneer life in
literature. 7. Women pioneers in literature. I. Miller, Dwight M.
II. Herbert Hoover Presidential Library and Museum.

PS3545.I342 Z763 2002
813'.52—dc21   2002018142 CIP

ISBN   978-0-7618-2285-1
ISBN 0-7618-2285-2 (paperback : alk. ppr.)

Contents

Copyright Permission

Introduction

ELIZABETH JAMESON

The essays in this volume originated as papers for the conference "Laura Ingalls Wilder and the American Frontier," hosted by the Herbert Hoover Presidential Library and Museum September 25-26, 1998. Historians, literary scholars, educators, and Little House fans gathered at the Presidential Library in West Branch, Iowa to discuss Wilder's vision of the American frontier, and her legacy in the more liminal frontiers of cultural exchange and collective memory. The conference itself occupied a cultural borderland of sorts, in which strong personal attachments to the Little House books coexisted with critical interpretations of Wilder's remarkable eight-volume autobiographical novel.

The speakers represented diverse approaches to Wilder and her work. Their essays appear here in the order in which they were originally presented. On the first day of the conference, John Miller, Ann Romines, Anita Clair Fellman, and Elizabeth Jameson approached Wilder's frontiers from the perspectives of biography, American history, American literature, women's studies, and western history. Ann Weller Dahl keynoted the second day, which was devoted to interpretations of Wilder's work in American classrooms and popular culture.

William T. Anderson, who moderated the conference, has recorded Ingalls and Wilder family history since the 1960s, leading a generation of scholars who have probed the connections between the Ingalls and Wilder families and the characters in the Little House Books who bear their names. Dwight Miller's essay, written for this volume, outlines how the papers of Laura Ingalls Wilder and Rose Wilder Lane came to be housed at the Hoover Presidential Library, where they helped lay the foundation for the research presented here.

The conference was an intellectual homecoming for the authors. We have all spent pleasant and productive hours exploring the Wilder and Lane papers in the supportive atmosphere provided by the Herbert Hoover Presidential Library staff and the citizens of West Branch. We want particularly to recognize and thank Dwight Miller, who provided extraordinary assistance to all of us over the years, and whose efforts made this book possible. It was gratifying to return to West Branch to share some of what we learned mining manuscripts in the archives.

Each of these papers grew from particular interests in Laura Ingalls Wilder and the world she wrote so indelibly. The growing body of Wilder scholarship testifies to the literary value and artistic appeal of the Little House books, and to their power to inscribe a particular vision of the pioneer past. Access to the Rose Wilder Lane and Laura Ingalls Wilder papers helped researchers explore how Wilder selected, filtered, and crafted her personal experience of western settlement into literature for children.

Over forty years after she left her South Dakota homestead, Laura Ingalls Wilder began to write her Little House series, the multi-volume children's novel based on her childhood. The eight volumes began with *Little House in the Big Woods*, published in 1932, and included *Farmer Boy* (1933), *Little House on the Prairie* (1935), *On the Banks of Plum Creek* (1937), *By the Shores of Silver Lake* (1939), *The Long Winter* (1940), *Little Town on the Prairie* (1941), and *These Happy Golden Years* (1943).[1] Through their pages, millions of readers met Laura Ingalls, her Ma and Pa, her sisters Mary, Carrie, and Grace, her husband Almanzo Wilder, and their wide supporting cast. The texts follow the Ingallses' pioneer journey from the Big Woods of Wisconsin to Indian Territory, to a farm on the Banks of Plum Creek near Walnut Grove, Minnesota, and, finally, to a homestead near the little town of De Smet, Dakota Territory. They end with Laura's marriage to Almanzo Wilder in the concluding chapters of *These Happy Golden Years*. By the time they wed, readers can feel familiar—even intimate—with the Wilder and Ingalls families.

In fact, the books offered crafted portions of the family histories from the years between 1866 (when Almanzo Wilder, the hero of *Farmer Boy*, was nine) until 1885, when Laura Ingalls and Almanzo Wilder married. Mrs. Wilder did not begin writing her books until she was over sixty, leading some to imagine a gifted and grandmotherly late bloomer, a literary Grandma Moses.[2] Readers knew very little about the relationship of the actual Ingalls and Wilder families to their fictional namesakes, and even less about the years after 1885. Mrs. Wilder did not encourage much interest in herself as a literary figure. Her daughter, Rose Wilder Lane, adamantly insisted on the literal truth of the books and discouraged researchers from probing discrepancies between the actual and fictional lives.[3]

Wilder enjoyed a quarter century of fame as a beloved children's author whose books, until well after she died in 1957, were widely accepted as literal autobiography, authenticated by the fact that Wilder used her own name and the names of her family and friends for the characters in her books. Since their factual accuracy was assumed, scholars and educators were primarily concerned with the literary devices and skill that drew readers so effectively into Laura's pioneer girlhood.

Louise Hovde Mortensen was one of the first to note a minor discrepancy in the dating of the Little House texts. Finding the Ingalls family listed on the 1870 census of Kansas, when the books' chronology would place them there in 1873, Mortensen suggested in 1964 that Wilder relied on her parents' accounts for some of her stories, and altered facts occasionally to improve her fiction.[4]

In the mid-1960s, William T. Anderson began his ambitious documentation of the Ingalls and Wilder families, and published the first results of his prodigious research.[5] Anderson probed small discrepancies between the Ingalls family's experience and the Little House stories and began to distinguish Laura Ingalls Wilder, the author and person, from the character Laura who bore her name. In an advance manuscript that Anderson sent to Rose Wilder Lane, he wrote that during the Ingalls family's first year in Dakota Territory they had "a few settlers as neighbors." That statement contradicted the fictional world of *By the Shores of Silver Lake*, where the family lived in isolation until Christmas Eve, when their future neighbors, Mr. and Mrs. Boast, arrived in the middle of a snowstorm. Lane, characteristically, resisted any inference that her mother's books were not absolute truth. "I object," she wrote Anderson, "to your statement that my mother was a liar. The Ingalls family spent their first winter in Dakota Territory approximately sixty miles from any neighbor." She modified her tone when she learned that Anderson was, at the time, thirteen years old, but continued to insist on the factual accuracy of the texts.[6]

Following the death of Rose Wilder Lane in 1967, her "adopted grandson" and executor, Roger Lea MacBride, published *The First Four Years*, a manuscript that Wilder had drafted in the mid-1930s and which differed in some details from the account of Laura and Almanzo's court-

ship and wedding in *These Happy Golden Years.*[7] The fact that Mrs. Wilder
told several versions of her own story opened questions about the literal
autobiographical accuracy of the Little House books. Rosa Ann Moore,
an English professor at the University of Tennessee, compared the published version of *The First Four Years* with the handwritten manuscripts
of *The Long Winter* and *These Happy Golden Years*, which Wilder had
donated to the Detroit Public Library. Recognizing that the manuscripts
differed in some significant ways from the published books, Moore explored the role of Rose Wilder Lane in editing, crafting, and marketing her
mother's books. Moore explored the role that Rose Wilder Lane played
in editing, crafting, and marketing her mother's books. Exploring "the
chemistry of collaboration" between mother and daughter, she dubbed the
Little House books "Rose colored classics."[8]

In 1976, Donald Zochert published the first book-length biography of Wilder.[9] He struggled, as her biographers must, with the difficulties posed by incomplete sources and the close identification of the author
with her fictional persona. Zochert's *Laura* was based in large measure
on the handwritten manuscript of Wilder's unpublished autobiographical
memoir, "Pioneer Girl," written between 1927 and 1930 for an adult audience.[10] Zochert also relied on newspapers and other public sources, and
on information and material provided by Roger Lea MacBride, William
Anderson, and by Irene Lichty, curator of the Laura Ingalls Wilder Home
and Museum in Mansfield, Missouri. As he distinguished the chronology
and experiences of her life from the accounts in the Little House books,
Zochert sought, he said, to tell Wilder's life "with honesty and affection."[11]

From all of these early efforts, some of Wilder's selective process
became apparent. The Ingalls family's pioneer journeys were simplified in
the Little House chronology, omitting in particular a period when the family
"backtracked" from Kansas Territory back to Wisconsin before journeying
to their farm near Walnut Grove, Minnesota, the site of *By the Banks of
Plum Creek*. Wilder also left out a difficult period in family history, from
1875-79, years that included the birth and death of Charles and Caroline
Ingallses' son, Charles Frederick, the loss of the Plum Creek farm, and the
family's move to Burr Oak, Iowa, where they helped run a hotel before
returning to Walnut Grove. Anderson and Zochert were able to document,
as well, the omission of two Wilder children from *Farmer Boy*, and other
alterations in factual detail as the lives were crafted into literature.[12]

A growing body of literary criticism followed Rosa Ann Moore's
path breaking efforts.[13] More complex analyses of the authorship of the
works and of Wilder herself, however, remained limited by access to

sources, until the Rose Wilder Lane papers, which included the Laura Ingalls Wilder collection, were deposited in the Herbert Hoover Presidential Library by Roger MacBride and opened to scholars beginning in 1980. (See Dwight Miller's essay in this volume). Lane left exponentially more written material to document her life, her work, and the mother-daughter relationship than did Wilder herself. It remains a challenge, as John Miller testifies in his essay, to tease Wilder's life from scattered and incomplete sources. Nonetheless, access to the Lane and Wilder papers marked a watershed for Little House scholarship.

Since the early 1980s, increasing numbers of writers have explored Wilder's maturation as an author, Wilder's and Lane's personal and professional relationships, the art of the Little House books themselves, and the messages they carry about history, gender, family, American values, and the West. Feminist literary criticism and new histories of women, settlement, and the American West, all provided new analytic tools and new lenses through which scholars viewed the intimate world of the Little House books. Anita Clair Fellman drew on feminist psychology for her influential 1990 interpretation of the politics of Wilder's and Lane's relationship. Both Fellman and Ann Romines became leading feminist interpreters of the Little House frontiers.[14] New approaches to the history of the American West and to American social history also provided new perspectives on Wilder's work. John Miller's 1994 history of De Smet, South Dakota, *Laura Ingalls Wilder's Little Town*, contributed not only to Wilder scholarship, but also to a new form of social history and community studies that emphasized daily life and community development. [15]

A generation of scholarship known collectively as the New Western History challenged histories of inexorable western progress in which the primary actors were white pioneers. These new histories emphasize interactions among immigrants of many racial and ethnic origins and American Indians. They replace celebratory tales of progress and expansion with plots based in conflict, conquest, accommodation, interaction with the natural environment, and the role of government in regional economies.[16] At the same time, new western women's histories recorded the diverse experiences of women in the American West, and further stimulated examinations of how race and gender affected social relationships and opportunity in the region.[17] As the historical cast and frontier narrative came under closer scrutiny, and as the players in the traditional frontier saga expanded to include women, immigrants, and people of diverse races, the plot that Wilder wrote was no longer the only obvious way to tell the story of western settlement. The Little House as a historical source and a historical narrative came under greater scrutiny. My own work falls into this category.[18]

My co-authors have long been recognized as leaders in the growing ferment of Wilder-Lane scholarship. For his article in this volume, John Miller draws on his recent biography, *Becoming Laura Ingalls Wilder,* to chronicle the challenges of teasing a life from limited sources, and to share some of his conclusions about how the girl Laura Ingalls *became* the author of the Little House books. Ann Romines' important feminist literary analysis of the Little House books, *Constructing the Little House: Gender, Culture, and Laura Ingalls Wilder,* draws on feminist criticism, culture studies, and new historicism. From those perspectives, she discusses how the Little House books engendered their own cultural frontiers. Anita Clair Fellman's forthcoming book, *The Little House Books in American Culture,* will provide the most thorough analysis to date of how historical contexts and social experiences affected how readers have understood the Little House books.[19] Educator Ann Weller Dahl is a leading exponent of how to teach the Little House books. Dwight Miller is more familiar than most Wilder scholars with the range of Wilder and Lane source material and what it can tell.

All of the authors participate in the ongoing conversations about literature, history, frontier, and gender to which the Little House books have contributed, and through which they have been read and interpreted. The exact role Lane played has been hotly debated since Moore penned her important essay, "Rose Colored Classics." The controversy reached a near boiling point following the 1993 publication of William Holtz's biography of Rose Wilder Lane, *The Ghost in the Little House.*[20] Holtz painted a grim picture of the mother-daughter relationship, and offered the strongest challenge to Wilder's authorship, suggesting that Lane was essentially her mother's ghostwriter. The dust has settled a bit since then. There is no longer any doubt that the books were the products of Wilder's and Lane's joint efforts. The authors in this volume generally adopt Moore's concept of "collaboration" to describe the relationship between Wilder as primary author and Lane as editor, adviser, and teacher. One strand of the ongoing conversation we engage in these pages addresses Rose Wilder Lane's influence: what parts of the books sprang from her typewriter, her historical imagination and political faith; which from her mother's pencil, memories, and her own sense of history and of the significance of the frontier past.

Some recent scholarship focuses less on who wrote what, and more on how the books themselves were embedded in conservative responses to the 1930s depression and the New Deal, on how those politics influenced the lessons that the books convey about family, self-sufficiency, and the pioneer past. Anita Clair Fellman, Fred Erisman, Janet Spaeth, and others have variously emphasized the values of self-reliance, family self-sufficiency, community, and faith in frontier progress that they find in Wilder's fiction, demonstrating in their own interpretations some of the values that readers have found in the books.[21] Ann Weller Dahl, who provides perhaps the most traditional reading of the books in this volume, offers an illuminating example of the interpretive process at work in her own classroom.

That interpretive process is an ongoing conversation that connects the Little House texts with each reader's life and history. Each of the authors of these essays has crossed boundaries of our own academic disciplines, of text and theory, and the subtle boundaries that divide our perspectives as Little House fans from the interpretive lenses through which we return to the texts. Our essays reflect a common effort to identify some of the filters through which the Little House books were written, and through which we understand them. Several themes unite these articles: themes of authorship, historical truth, audience, and memory.

The first theme is the connection of authors to their work. We acknowledge the questions posed by the role of Rose Wilder Lane, herself a popular fiction writer, in her mother's literary apprenticeship, and in the writing and editing of the Little House books. We address as well the relationship of Laura Ingalls Wilder, the person and author, to her literary persona and to the Little House character. Adding another layer to this interpretive question, most of us also address our own relationships to the Little House books, acknowledging our personal involvements with the texts, and the intellectual and personal vantage points from which we write.

The second theme involves the relationship between fiction and history. What changed as Laura Ingalls Wilder crafted her own life into fiction for children? Did those changes affect the human or the historical truth of the books? How did the passage of time—the fact that Wilder wrote the books during the 1930s Depression and World War II, when she was in her 60s and early 70s—affect the message she wrote for her young readers? In what ways does the Little House represent an actual pioneer past, and how accurately does the particular world of the Little House books represent a more general frontier experience?

These questions are not easy. The Little House books are eloquent testimony to how hard it is to distinguish truth and fiction. Literature—fiction—can convey essential human and historical truths. And histories are themselves narratives, with chosen characters, plots, chronologies, and action. Histories are crafted, interpreted, revised. The connections between history and culture, and the diverse ways people remember and record the past, can lead to more interesting questions than who wrote what, to more complex and less certain assessments of the meanings and values we find on the Little House frontiers.

The third common theme of these essays is the relationship between author and audience. Readers enter the Little Houses through different doors: the images of childhood, family, gender, and the West that various readers bring to the books have changed over time. History and cultural contexts have affected how generations of readers have read the Little House books. Those changes, quite beyond the reach of the author and her intent, also shed new light on changing interpretations of American identity and of the frontier.

These three-shared themes link a series of relationships: the relationship of the author to her text, of the text to history, and of the audience to a work of art. The looping conversations between author and reader, between past and present, lie at the core of these essays, to connect their diverse approaches and differing conclusions. The larger theme of memory animates each article—how Laura Ingalls Wilder remembered her life, how subsequent generations remembered her, how her memory informed her art, how her work has been interpreted and remembered over time, and how the Little House books have been written into a collective memory of a pioneer past.

The Laura Ingalls Wilder and the American Frontier conference mirrored, as a cultural event, many of these themes and connections. It generated conversations across generations of readers and across disciplines; it bridged academic and popular interests and discourses; it crossed boundaries of time and memory. The audience included people of all ages and backgrounds and represented a broad sample of the millions of readers who have entered the Little Houses since 1932. Some had family ties to the characters in the Little House books; some were educators; some were teachers and scholars of American history and culture; some were simply fascinated with the pioneer past.

Most of us, presenters and audience alike, have revisited Laura Ingalls Wilder and her family over many years. We have read and re-read the Little House books, charting changes in own lives as we returned over time to treasured childhood stories. This dense web of Little House connections took us beyond a simple celebration of Laura Ingalls Wilder's pioneer experience as recorded in the Little House books, to suggest some of the disparate windows the Little Houses open on American history, identity, and art. Yet, precisely because the Little House frontier is familiar and beloved territory, it presents particular challenges for interpretation. Analyzing the significance of the Little House books may seem like questioning eternal verities or interrogating one's grandmother. The compelling pulls of patriotism, of inherited histories of westward expansion, the appeals of strong families and secure childhoods, the nostalgic attractions of a mythic frontier, all combine to generate respectful but not always comfortable examinations of the Little House saga.

The conference format reflected those pulls, and a difficult divide in the popular culture that surrounds the Little House. The scholars presented the first day. The second day was devoted to how the books are read and enacted in popular venues. The ways the stories have been read are complicated by popular culture. Historic sites and museums commemorate the scenes of the Little House books and the lives of the Ingalls and Wilder families. A variety of spin-off books and Little House memorabilia generate their own Little House filters. The "Little House on the Prairie" television series, which ran from 1974-83, introduced many viewers to the books through filtered plots and through characters who differ significantly from their counterparts in the books and in history. The commercial nostalgia that surrounds some of these Little Houses is often far removed from serious historic preservation and scholarship, and equally far from the world of Laura Ingallses' childhood.

It is difficult and sometimes wrenching to separate nostalgia and myth from the significance of real lives, history, and art. That is the challenge of the Little House frontier. The authors of these essays approach this challenge from separate vantage points, and reach no simple or common conclusions. The effort to untangle the legacies of the Little House frontiers is the common ground from which we write. That continuing conversation between past and present, between personal lives and collective memories, constitutes perhaps the most intriguing, continuous, and enduring inheritance of the Little House frontier.

Endnotes

1. Laura Ingalls Wilder, *Little House in the Big Woods* (New York: Harper & Brothers Publishers, 1932); *Farmer Boy* (New York: Harper & Brothers Publishers, 1933); *Little House on the Prairie* (New York: Harper & Brothers Publishers, 1935); *On the Banks of Plum Creek* (New York: Harper & Brothers Publishers, 1937); *By the Shores of Silver Lake* (New York: Harper & Brothers Publishers, 1939); *The Long Winter* (New York: Harper & Brothers Publishers, 1940); *Little*

Town on the Prairie (New York: Harper & Brothers Publishers, 1941); *These Happy Golden Years* (New York: Harper & Brothers Publishers, 1943).

2. For accounts of Wilder's previous literary efforts and her maturation as an author, see William T. Anderson, "The Literary Apprenticeship of Laura Ingalls Wilder," *South Dakota History* 13 (Summer 1983): 285-331; "Laura Ingalls Wilder and Rose Wilder Lane: The Continuing Collaboration," *South Dakota History* 16 (Winter 1986): 89-143; and John E. Miller, *Becoming Laura Ingalls Wilder: The Woman Behind the Legend* (Columbia and London: University of Missouri Press, 1998).

3. See Anderson, "Literary Apprenticeship," 286-89. One slice of Wilder's experience on the journey from De Smet to the Wilder's new home in Mansfield, Missouri became available with the publication of Wilder's diary from that journey in 1962. See Wilder, *On the Way Home: The Diary of a Trip from South Dakota to Mansfield, Missouri, in 1894* (New York: Harper & Row, Publishers, 1962).

4. Louise Hovde Mortensen, "Idea Inventory," *Elementary English* 41 (April 1964): 428-29.

5. Anderson, who began his research as an elementary school student, published his first pamphlet about the Ingalls family in 1967; see William T. Anderson, *The Story of the Ingalls* (1967; revised ed., De Smet, S.D.: Laura Ingalls Wilder Memorial Society, 1993). His subsequent publications include: *Laura Wilder of Mansfield* (De Smet, S.D.: Laura Ingalls Wilder Memorial Society, 1968; 1982 ed.); *A Wilder in the West: the Story of Eliza Jane Wilder* (De Smet, S.D.: Laura Ingalls Wilder Memorial Society, 1971; 1985 ed.); *The Story of the Wilders* (Davison, Michigan: Anderson Publications, 1972; 1983 ed.); *"Laura's Rose": The Story of Rose Wilder Lane* (De Smet, S.D.: Laura Ingalls Wilder Memorial Society, 1968; Centennial Edition, 1986); *Laura Ingalls Wilder; The Iowa Story* (Burr Oak, Iowa: Laura Ingalls Wilder Park & Museum, 1990); *Laura Ingalls Wilder: A Biography* (New York: HarperCollins Publishers, 1992).

6. See Anderson, "Literary Apprenticeship," 288-89; letter from Rose Wilder Lane to William T. Anderson, 30 June 1966, quoted 288.

7. Wilder, *The First Four Years* (New York:Harper & Row, Publishers, 1971). Anderson, "The Literary Apprenticeship," makes the case that the manuscript was drafted between 1933 and 1937, rather than after *These Happy Golden Years*, shortly before Almanzo Wilder died in 1949, as MacBride guessed in his introduction *The First Four Years*, xiv. On differences between the two books, see for instance Janet Spaeth, *Laura Ingalls Wilder* (Boston: Twayne Publishers, 1987) 68-71.

8. Rosa Ann Moore, "Laura Ingalls Wilder's Orange Notebooks and the Art of the Little House Books," *Children's Literature*, 4 (1975): 105-19; "Laura Ingalls Wilder and Rose Wilder Lane: The Chemistry of Collaboration," *Children's Literature in Education* (Autumn 1980): 101-9; and "The Little House Books: Rose-Colored Classics," *Children's Literature* 7 (1978): 7-16.

9. Donald Zochert, *Laura: The Life of Laura Ingalls Wilder* (Chicago: Henry Regnery Company, 1976).

10. Laura Ingalls Wilder wrote her draft of "Pioneer Girl" between 1927-1930; Rose Wilder Lane typed several drafts and submitted them to agents. Copies sent to Carl Brandt and George T. Bye are in the Rose Wilder Lane Papers, Laura Ingalls Wilder Series, Herbert Hoover Presidential Library, West Branch Iowa.

11. Zochert, *Laura*, "Preface," 10.

12. For the story of these years, see Zochert, *Laura*, 103-46; Anderson, *The Story of the Ingalls*, 6-8; *Laura Ingalls Wilder*, 62-88; *Laura Ingalls Wilder; The Iowa Story*; and Miller, *Becoming Laura Ingalls Wilder*, 31-44.

13. See Elizabeth Segel, "Laura Ingalls Wilder's America: An Unflinching Assessment," *Children's Literature in Education* 8 (1977): 63-70; Anna Thompson Lee, "'It Is Better Farther On': Laura Ingalls Wilder and the Pioneer Spirit," *The Lion and the Unicorn* 3 (1979): 74-88; Hamida Bosmajian, "Vastness and Contractions of Space in *Little House on the Prairie*," *Children's Literature* 11 (1983): 49-63; William Holtz, "Closing the Circle: the American Optimism of Laura Ingalls Wilder," *Great Plains Quarterly* 4 (1984): 79-90; Kathryn Adam, "Laura, Ma, Mary, Carrie, and Grace: Western Women as Portrayed by Laura Ingalls Wilder," in Susan Armitage and Elizabeth Jameson, eds., *The Women's West* (Norman: University of Oklahoma Press, 1987), 95-110; Spaeth, *Laura Ingalls Wilder*. For earlier criticism, see *The Horn Book Magazine*, December 1953 (special Laura Ingalls Wilder issue); Wilbur Jay Jacobs, "Frontier Faith Revisited: The Little House Books of Laura Ingalls Wilder," *The Horn Book Magazine* 5 (October 1965): 472-73.

14. Anita Clair Fellman, "Laura Ingalls Wilder and Rose Wilder Lane: The Politics of a Mother-Daughter Relationship," *Signs: Journal of Women in Culture and Society* 15:3 (1990): 535-61; "Everybody's 'Little Houses': Reviewers and Critics Read Laura Ingalls Wilder," *Publishing Research Quarterly* 12:1 (Spring 1996): 3-19; "'Don't Expect to Depend on Anybody Else': The Frontier as Portrayed in the Little House Books," *Children's Literature* 24, ed. R.H.W. Dillard and Elizabeth Lennox Keyser (New Haven: Yale University Press, 1996; copyright Hollins College), 101-116; Ann Romines, "The Long Winter: An Introduction to Western Womanhood," *Great Plains Quarterly* 80 (Winter 1990): 36-47; *Constructing the Little House: Gender, Culture, and Laura Ingalls Wilder* (Amherst: University of Massachusetts Press, 1997).

15. John E. Miller, *Laura Ingalls Wilder's Little Town: Where History and Literature Meet* (Lawrence: University Press of Kansas, 1994).

16. The New Western History refers to a large body of work published since the 1980s and tracing its roots to a generation of revisionist interpretations beginning in the 1960s. It supports many interpretations and has sparked considerable internal debate among western historians, including those considered new western historians. For representative works and useful references, see Patricia Nelson Limerick, *The Legacy of Conquest: The Unbroken Past of the American West* (New York: W. W. Norton & Company, 1987); Richard White, *It's Your Misfortune and None of My Own: A New History of the American West* (Norman: Uni-

versity of Oklahoma Press, 1991); Patricia Nelson Limerick, Clyde A, Milner II, and Charles Rankin, eds., *Trails: Toward a New Western History* (Lawrence: University Press of Kansas, 1991); and William Cronon, George Miles, and Jay Gitlin, eds., *Under an Open Sky* (New York: W. W. Norton & Company, 1992). For works that emphasize differences of race and gender, see Quintard Taylor, *In Search of the Racial Frontier: African Americans in the American West, 1528-1990* (New York: W.W. Norton & Company, 1998); Sucheng Chan, Douglas Henry Daniels, Mario T. Garcia, and Terry P. Wilson, eds., *Peoples of Color in the American West* (Lexington, Mass.: D.C. Heath and Company, 1994); Elizabeth Jameson and Susan Armitage, eds., *Writing the Range: Race, Class, and Color in the Women's West* (Norman: University of Oklahoma Press, 1997). For useful histories of pioneer childhood, see Elliott West, *Growing Up With the Country* (Albuquerque: University of New Mexico Press, 1989) and Elizabeth Hampsten, *Settlers' Children* (Norman: University of Oklahoma Press, 1991). For a consideration of Wilder's frontiers from historical perspectives, see Fred Erisman, *Laura Ingalls Wilder*, Boise State University Western Writers Series Number 112 (Boise, Idaho: Boise State University, 1994). For an important critical response to the books from an American Indian perspective, see Michael Dorris, "Trusting the Words," *Booklist* (June 1 & 15, 1993): 1820-22.

17. Western women's history as a field is generally dated from one article, Joan M. Jensen and Darlis A. Miller, "The Gentle Tamers Revisited: New Approaches to the History of Women in the American West," *Pacific Historical Review* 49:2 (May 1980): 173-213, and from two conferences, the Women's West Conference in Sun Valley, Idaho, August 10-13, 1983, and Western Women: Their Land, Their Lives, Tucson, Arizona, January 12-15, 1984. The conferences generated two anthologies, Armitage and Jameson, eds., *The Women's West*, and Lillian Schlissel, Vicki L. Ruiz, and Janice Monk, eds., *Western Women: Their Lives, Their Land* (Albuquerque: University of New Mexico Press, 1988). For reviews of some of this early scholarship, see Jensen and Miller, "The Gentle Tamers Revisited," and Elizabeth Jameson, "Toward a Multicultural History of Women in the Western United States," *Signs* 13:4 (Summer 1988): 761-91.

18. See Jameson, "In Search of the Great Ma," *Journal of the West* 37:2 (April 1998): 42-52. This work is influenced as well by feminist literary criticism, particularly Carolyn G. Heilbrun, *Writing a Woman's Life* (New York: Ballantine Books, 1988).

19. Miller, *Becoming Laura Ingalls Wilder*; Romines, *Constructing the Little House*; Fellman, *The Little House Books in American Culture: The Literature of Individualism* (forthcoming, University of Illinois Press; title provisional).

20. William Holtz, *The Ghost in the Little House: A Life of Rose Wilder Lane* (Columbia: University of Missouri Press, 1993).

21. Fellman, "'Don't Expect to Depend on Anybody Else'"; Lee, "It Is Better Farther On'"; Holtz, "Closing the Circle"; Spaeth, *Laura Ingalls Wilder*; Jacobs, "Frontier Faith Revisited"; Erisman, *Laura Ingalls Wilder*.

Approaching Laura Ingalls Wilder: Challenges and Opportunities for the Biographer

JOHN E. MILLER

At first glance, writing a biography of Laura Ingalls Wilder might seem to pose a simple task. What could be too complicated about it? Or about her, for that matter? This simple farm woman, living in the Missouri Ozarks, taking up her pen—or, rather, her pencil—at the age of sixty-five to write a popular series of autobiographical novels aimed at young readers. The first one published to immediate acclaim, the others arriving regularly every two or three years, each one winning plaudits from reviewers and readers alike. Laura Ingalls Wilder—beloved children's author, recalling scenes from her childhood and adolescence, her story culminating in her marriage to Almanzo Wilder. A posthumously published novel bringing the narrative forward through the first four years of their marriage. This, a story of the frontier, of a spunky, independent-minded girl and young woman, her personality shaped in somewhat equal proportions by her "Pa," Charles Ingalls, and her "Ma," Caroline Ingalls, although she seemed in many ways more the child of her father, with his "itchy" foot and impetuousness, than of her mother, with her calm and well-regulated demeanor.

What could be so hard about writing a biography of this woman? We have her stories, preserved so wonderfully in her books, the first one published when she was sixty-five. We have the testimony of her adoring readers. We can trace her family's wanderings from place to place, and we can return to visit the sites and put her story into historical context.

All of this might seem simple enough, in a way, but as soon as we tackle the assignment, questions and problems quickly start emerging. The question generating the most attention lately is the one of authorship. Who really wrote the books? How large a role did Wilder's daughter, Rose Wilder Lane, play in the process? Might she, in fact, have been the ghost-writer of the books?[1] Assuming that her mother played the sole or, at least, primary role in constructing the novels, the question arises of how this seemingly simple woman, with no previous fiction-writing experience, could have created such wonderful stories that remain today best-sellers and are recognized as some of the best children's literature ever written in this country. Other questions demand attention. What kind of person was Laura, really? What were the influences upon her personality and character? What was the nature of her relationship with her husband, Almanzo? More interestingly, what about her daughter, and only child, Rose? What could have driven this brilliantly precocious child to say later in life that her childhood had been "a nightmare" and that her mother "made me so miserable when I was a child that I've never gotten over it"?[2]

Beyond that, other questions come to the fore. What was the nature of the frontier that Wilder grew up in? What kinds of communities did her family live in? How was Mansfield, Missouri, her home for the last sixty-three years of her life, similar to or different from what she had known as a child and young woman? What kind of identity did Laura carve out for herself as an adult? What occupied her time? What were her ideas, beliefs, and values? Perhaps most of all, what kinds of ambitions did she have, and how did she attempt to fulfill them? She had written an essay on the subject of ambition as a high schooler, later incorporating it (in modified form) in one of her books, *These Happy Golden Years*. If ambition set her apart from other Ozark farmwomen, how did that ambition play itself out in Wilder's life?

Beyond that, where did she acquire the competence to write her novels? How could this supposedly "untutored housewife in the Ozarks" transform herself so suddenly into one of America's best-known and most beloved children's authors? What stimulated her to write? How did she go about doing it? What was the process involved? And what did she think about it while she was doing it?

Posing such questions is not such a difficult task. They arise naturally during the process of thinking about and researching the subject. It is a mite harder to answer them. The biggest problem facing any researcher of Laura Ingalls Wilder is to find sources that reveal very much about her personality and her manner of thinking. This problem is set in high relief by the fact that her daughter, unlike her, unloaded reams of gut-wrenching, revelatory comments about her thoughts, feelings, doubts, aspirations, dreams, desires, and musings on life. Rose sporadically kept diaries and journals into which she often poured her darkest fears and resentments. And she was in the habit of writing six-, seven-, and eight-page, single-spaced, typewritten letters to friends and correspondents, constituting a sort of psycho-autobiography of herself. For Rose, writing letters created a kind of surrogate family and constituted a form of self-therapy. For her mother, little of this kind of material exists. There are no diaries, aside from the account of her and Almanzo's journey from South Dakota to Missouri in 1894.[3] There are no gut-spilling journals. There are a limited number of letters, the most revealing being those written when she was traveling, as on her visit to Rose in San Francisco in 1915 or when she and Rose were collaborating on her books after Rose had moved away from Rocky Ridge. The task for the biographer of Laura Ingalls Wilder thus becomes one of piecing together information from a variety of sources, which directly or indirectly throw light on her life and career.

Lest this starts to sound too gloomy, however, it should be noted that several wonderful sources assist immeasurably in the task. We have the handwritten drafts not only of the novels but also of Wilder's autobiography, "Pioneer Girl," written in 1930. There are also typewritten drafts of the books in various forms, allowing us to observe the progress being made as Wilder's original version was transformed into final published form. Rose took her mother's hand-written drafts and "ran them through her typewriter." She then attacked them herself with pen and ink, and Laura made her own penciled corrections and changes. During the period when Rose was living at Rocky Ridge, the two were able to talk back and forth with each other. After she moved away in 1935, they had to communicate at a distance. For several of the books (*On the Banks of Plum Creek, By the Shores of Silver Lake,* and *The Long Winter*) there is extensive correspondence between the two as they discussed and argued about how to proceed in revising the manuscripts. Most of the letters that were saved are ones from Laura to Rose, but there are a few from Rose to Laura. In this correspondence we can observe most clearly the process of collaboration that occurred between the two.

Another source of prime importance in researching my biography was the columns that Laura wrote for the *Missouri Ruralist,* beginning in 1911. Beyond that, much of the social and historical context for the lives of Laura and Almanzo Wilder is contained in the local newspaper, the *Mansfield Mirror* after 1908. Some scattered issues of predecessor newspapers are available. Unfortunately, most of the newspapers before 1908 have been lost. Many of the facts about Wilder's life in Mansfield in my biography come directly from newspaper columns. I also used the newspaper to sketch a picture of life in the town and the Ozarks, noting that Laura and Almanzo may or may not have participated in the activities that are being described.

In addition to these important sources, a variety of other primary sources are useful, both for pinning down facts about Wilder and her family directly and for delineating the context in which she lived. These include census records, land and deed records, probate records, county histories, personal memoirs, interviews, and the like. Fortunately, there are also still some people who can personally recall Laura and Almanzo and other members of her family. Among the people I was able to talk to, Neta Seal, who, along with her husband Silas, joined Laura and Almanzo on their trip to the West Coast in 1938 and became fast friends with the Wilders during the last years of their lives, had the most information to impart. The most interesting thing I learned from Wilder's friends and acquaintances came from the librarian, Nava Austin, who revealed that Laura's favorite reading matter consisted of westerns, especially those written by Luke Short and Zane Grey.

Beyond the relative paucity of primary sources, another challenge awaits any prospective Wilder biographer. Some of the most useful sources present the information through the lens of her daughter, Rose. Most of what we know about the 1920s and 1930s comes from Rose's letters, diaries, and journals. The best insights into the often strained and frequently tortuous relationship between mother and daughter derive from what Rose wrote. Accepting these sources uncritically would result in a lop-sided view of the interaction between the two. Caution is called for in interpreting what Rose had to say about her mother.

Wilder's biographer faces other challenges, one being that most readers bring strong preconceptions along with them in approaching the subject. People who contemplate Wilder's life usually have already formed opinions about her based upon reading the novels and perhaps also from viewing the television programs, which, it should be said, have very little relation to the novels that Wilder wrote, as I am sure most of you would agree. Ideally, students of Wilder should cast aside these preconceptions and view the evidence afresh. More realistically, perhaps, they should at least be willing to set aside temporarily their preconceptions and let the evidence take them where it will.

The final problem that I was always aware of in pursuing the research was my own background as a historian rather than as a literary analyst. My original impulse in studying Wilder was to ask how her novels could help us understand the history of family and community on the frontier. Only later did I turn my focus on her as an author. Some may perceive in my book a naive effort to establish facts where a factual accounting is unobtainable. In the minds of some literary critics, literature is more a matter of textuality than factuality. The search for historical fact, some would contend, is a futile exercise, doomed before it starts. Aware of the difficulty of my task, however, I persist in trying to pin down the facts with the highest degree of probability and let it go at that.

My attempt to analyze and interpret Wilder's writings came in an earlier book, *Laura Ingalls Wilder's Little Town: Where History and Literature Meet.* There I took my cue from Lionel Trilling, who grounded his literary criticism on the premise that the novel "is a perpetual quest for reality, the field of its research being always the social world." This biography seeks to understand and explain the woman who wrote the novels. The task is a challenging one. A biographer, Leon Edel notes, "must be warm, yet aloof, involved, yet uninvolved. To be cold as ice in appraisal, yet warm and human and understanding, this is the biographer's dilemma."[4]

Always, our vision is partial; the portrait that we paint is one of many that can be presented. Doris Kearns Goodwin observes about the process of biographical research:

> "We rummage through letters, memos, pictures, memories, diaries, and conversations in an attempt to develop our subject's character from youth to [adult]hood to death. Yet, in the end, if we are honest with ourselves, the best we can offer is a partial rendering, a subjective portrait of the subject from a particular angle of vision shaped as much by our own biography—our attitudes, perceptions, and feelings toward the subject—as by the raw material themselves."[5]

My assumption in approaching the task, contrary to those who would proclaim "the death of the author," is that the author, in this case, was very much alive. If she required assistance in writing the books from Rose, she was very much involved in the process herself, and, in delineating the process of collaboration that occurred between the two, we enhance our understanding of the books.

The subtitle of my book, "The Woman Behind the Legend," implies that part of the task of any researcher into Wilder's life is to clear away the underbrush of myth and legend that has come to surround her. In my introduction, I note that the "myths that have endured about the 'nice old lady' who lived and wrote in the farmhouse up on the hill at Rocky Ridge may stand in the way of looking at her with open eyes."[6] I don't really dwell on the legend that has grown up around Wilder over the years. Instead, I take its presence for granted and focus my efforts on telling the story of Wilder's life as simply and truthfully as I can. Some day someone will come along and show in detail, as best as can be established, the discrepancies that exist between the stories that Wilder told and her life as lived. That, however, would take another book; it is not the one that I wrote.

The more important message of this biography is contained in the first word of the title, *Becoming Laura Ingalls Wilder*. The word "becoming" is important because Wilder's life was a continuous process of change and development.[7] It was not a fluke or coincidence that she did not begin writing the books until she was in her early sixties. She probably would have been incapable of doing it earlier. I see Wilder as undergoing a process of training—mostly self-training—between the ages of forty-four, when she started writing her farm newspaper columns, and sixty-three, when she sat down to write her autobiography.

In writing her biweekly column for the *Missouri Ruralist*, Wilder acquired a habit of turning out words on a regular basis to meet a deadline and of thinking through ideas and concepts and translating them into stories and descriptions that carried with them some kind of point or moral. She learned how to use and manipulate words so they would have the most effect. Some of her columns derived from childhood memories and related stories that were later incorporated into her novels. In this way, she began to practice writing the kind of narrative that she later honed to a high degree in fictional form.[8]

The Wilder who was lionized as a children's author during the nineteen thirties and 'forties was the culmination of a process combining elements of ambition, skill, experience, drive, and determination. A lesser woman would have given up the quest part way through; satisfied with the success she had already achieved or would not have made the attempt at all. Without her daughter Rose's encouragement and prodding as well as her substantial assistance in revising the manuscripts, the books would certainly never have seen the light of day.

The "becoming" that I am talking about here was also reflected in the names that were associated with Wilder over the years. As a child, she was her father's little "flutterbudget" and "half-pint of cider half-drunk up." As a schoolgirl, she was "Laura." To her fiancé and soon-to-be husband Almanzo Wilder, she was "Bessie"; to her daughter Rose, "Mama

Bess." To the world at large as a young, married woman, she was "Laura Wilder." Mostly, during her adult life, especially in stories in the local newspaper, she was "Mrs. A. J. Wilder," making her as much or more the wife of her husband as an independent woman in her own right. But "Laura Ingalls Wilder," the tag that made her famous, and that we think of her as, was hardly ever associated with her before her first book was published with that as her pen name. (Several magazine articles written in the 1920s identified her as Laura Ingalls Wilder, but her columns in the *Missouri Ruralist* all went under the name of Mrs. A. J. Wilder.) As a book author, Laura was not simply the wife of her husband; she became a person of some importance. She was Laura Ingalls Wilder—carrying the Ingalls family heritage with her, a farmwoman who lived in the Ozarks of Missouri, an experienced farm journalist and all that that entailed.

One of my major goals in writing this book was to show that Laura Ingalls Wilder was much more than a book author and that her many and varied activities made her an interesting and significant woman, aside from her writing. She was a deeply religious person, despite the fact that she and her husband never formally joined the Methodist church in Mansfield. With no Congregational church in town, they had to settle for another Protestant denomination that resembled it. Wilder's religiosity showed itself more in her personal everyday life than in her connection to formal religion, although she was for many years a steady churchgoer and participant in the Methodist Ladies Aid. References in her books to church activities and Bible-reading, a handwritten list of Bible verses that she kept close at hand in her Bible, and comments that she made in letters and talks all testify to the genuineness of her faith and the importance of religion in her life.

Wilder's politics were somewhat more problematic. We know that she was a Democrat in the beginning, that she continued to be associated with the party during the 1920s, and that she even was involved in a leadership position as chair of the Wright County Democratic Committee.[9] Wilder ran for a local office in 1925, Collector of Pleasant Valley Township, a contest that she lost. (Rose thought the election had been stolen from her.) Sometime during the late 1920s or early 1930s Wilder's party affiliation changed, and she and Almanzo, like their daughter, became staunch critics and opponents of Franklin Roosevelt and the New Deal. While her political views can accurately be described as "arch-conservative" during the 1930s and till the end of her life, she never went to the extremes that Rose did in her hatred of Roosevelt and in her attachment to libertarian thinking. Also, unlike Rose, whose political thought can be extensively documented from her published and unpublished writings, Wilder said or wrote little that would indicate much about the details of her thinking on the subject.

Wilder's political orientation is a topic worth further investigation. To what degree do Wilder's novels reflect her conservative—or, better, "independent"—political views? Wilder was an advocate of individualism and freedom, but she was also devoted to community. Family was important to her, and family constitutes a central component of community.

Wilder herself, in the Tocquevillian tradition, was an avid joiner and participant in organizations and in community life. Beyond her involvement in the Methodist church and in the Democratic Party, she helped organize and served for many years as secretary-treasurer of the Mansfield branch of the National Farm Loan Association, a job of considerable responsibility and trust. She actively participated in and worked to promote the Mansfield Agricultural and Stock Show. Along with Almanzo, she was a member of the Eastern Star, carrying on the tradition of her father, whose Masonic emblem was carved on his tombstone. But most importantly she was an active clubwoman, helping organize and participating extensively in a variety of different clubs over the years.

Some of these organizations were geared mostly to entertainment and conviviality, like the embroidery club and the bridge clubs that she belonged to. Others were part of the extensive women's self-education movement that had grown during the nineteenth and early twentieth centuries. Wilder wrote approvingly in her *Missouri Ruralist* column about the increasing importance of such study clubs in the 1910s. She became a charter member of and enthusiastic participant in the Athenian Club, which was organized in 1916 by a group of women, mostly from the Hartville area. She was one of the few farmwomen to become a member. Her participation in it and other clubs often brought her into contact with the wives of important store owners, lawyers, bankers, and other local luminaries who collectively constituted the local "power elite" of small town Missouri. Later on, she played a prominent role in the Justamere Club, the Interesting Hour Club, the Friday Afternoon Club, and several embroidery and bridge clubs.

These study clubs performed a serious educational function. Discussion topics for their meetings ranged from Russian Communism and the Panama Canal to prominent people, social customs, and the birds of South America. But they also provided social outlets for their members and helped reinforce community bonds. The Wilders also entertained groups of friends at their farmhouse at Rocky Ridge and in a variety of ways participated actively in community life. Yet the nature of their involvement remains sketchy. We would like to know more about the full range of activities that they participated in and the extensiveness of them. There always remained some distance between Wilder and the town. This might relate, in part to their being latecomers from South Dakota. To some degree, at least, she and her husband always remained a little different from their neighbors. Their family roots were in New England, while most residents in the area traced their origins to Tennessee, Kentucky, Virginia, and North Carolina. Wilder's personality and behavior also factored into her relations with others. Living in the margin between town and country gave her something of a split identity. Unlike other farmwomen, she refused to go into town in a plain gingham dress but always tried to dress up a little. This, in the view of some people, made her seem a little "hoity-toity," distant, or even "prissy." Also involved, no doubt, was the fact that she was better read and more ambitious than most of her neighbors, and she conceived of herself as being different somehow from them.

With all of her activities; with a husband with whom she was compatible, although they had their share of fights and bickering; with a daughter who engendered pride and wonderment in them, but also disappointed them when she failed to remarry and live a more conventional lifestyle; and with generally supportive friends and neighbors, Laura Ingalls Wilder lived a meaningful and satisfying life. But with the publication, between the ages of sixty-five and seventy-six of eight novels that made her increasingly famous, she emerged as a woman of some importance in twentieth century literature. A small Wilder "industry" developed over time, with many articles about her writing being published in newspapers and magazines and in scholarly journals. Historians have jumped on the bandwagon and taken the novels seriously as sources of the social history of the frontier.

Of late, a mild Wilder "boom" has occurred. New fictional series by Roger MacBride and Maria Wilkes about Wilder's daughter and mother have enjoyed considerable success. William Anderson, Janet Spaeth, Donald Zochert, Anita Clair Fellman, and others have done much to enhance our understanding of both Wilder and her writing. Ann Romines' new interpretive study provides the most comprehensive analysis of Wilder's novels and will stimulate further research. With the deposit of the Rose Wilder Lane papers by her informally adopted grandson, Roger MacBride, at the Hoover Presidential Library, the opportunity for intensive research in the manuscripts, letters, and documents of Lane and her mother became possible. Rosa Ann Moore was the first researcher to demonstrate that, rather than being solely the work of Wilder, the books resulted from a collaborative process between mother and daughter. William Anderson has also gone into considerable detail on the writing process; in addition, he remains the most knowledgeable expert about all aspects of Wilder's writing and life.

The most explosive and controversial interpretation of Wilder's personality and work came with the publication of William Holtz's biography of Lane in 1993, titled *The Ghost in the Little House*. In it, Holtz argues that Wilder remained an amateurish writer to the end and that almost everything we admire about her books resulted from Lane's "fine touch."[10] In effect, Holtz contends that Lane ghostwrote the novels. While some reviewers were quick to accept his argument, the consensus seems to be veering in the other direction. Any biographer of Wilder must necessarily confront this issue head-on.

One thing I did in my research was to read Wilder's handwritten manuscripts side by side with the finished books and attempt to find where they coincided and where they differed. I took a red pen and marked in the books where the language rather closely followed the original language in Wilder's manuscript. Green ink was used to indicate places that obviously had been inserted, or added, or seriously modified, the assumption being that Rose probably was responsible for most of the new language. Where there was no red or green ink in the margins, I was not able to figure out exactly where the material had come from. Suffice it to say there are large segments in all of the books where there is a lot of red ink. There are many places where green ink is present. And then there are large sections also where there is no ink. It would take someone with more time and patience than I to sort all of this out and then to go through all of the available intermediate manuscripts that are at the Hoover Library and trace, as best one can, how the changes were made. As I indicate in my introduction, "There certainly is room for scholars to make a systematic study of the manuscripts and to describe in detail where changes were made and—to the degree that it can be ascertained—determine who was responsible for what in the final outcome."[11]

In addition to the manuscripts, we have letters back and forth between Wilder and Lane, while they were working on several of the novels, arguing as well as agreeing over how to proceed in particular instances with the revisions. And we have Rose's diary for at least part of the period, in which she notes—day by day—what she was doing in the process of revising *Little House in the Big Woods, Farmer Boy, Little House on the Prairie*, and the other books. We can establish with a fair degree of accuracy at least the time spans during which she was working on most of them.

Taking all of this together, I join with those who attribute primary importance to Wilder as the author of her novels. While Lane's contribution was significant, the vast majority of the story lines, episodes, characters, and language came from her mother. As Rose said, her mother was excellent at description but not so practiced at structure. As a result, a fair amount of rearranging occurred in several books. Lane also sometimes took a paragraph or a page and expanded it into several paragraphs or pages. She did a large amount of revising, expanding, rearranging, and rewriting the books. Aristotelian logic—which divides everything into "A" or "not-A," requiring either/or answers—fails us here. An infusion of "fuzzy" logic is called for.[12] Responsibility for the books needs to be attributed to *both* mother and daughter, but I will stick with the former as having primary importance. If it helps our understanding to put things in terms of percentages, I'd estimate it as being about 70% Laura and 30% Rose. I think we get hung up too much on labels. But as long as we are going to use them, I will continue to attach "author" to Wilder and "collaborator"—rather than "ghostwriter"—to Lane.

Many other topics deserve further investigation. I think my biography answers or throws new light upon a lot of questions. But I expect many more articles and books to be written about Wilder. The kinds of questions that remain at issue or that need to be addressed in future research include the following:

One more time—who wrote the books, or who deserves primary credit for their authorship? There is much more that can be done, on a book-by-book basis, to explain the process of collaboration that occurred between mother and daughter in the writing of the novels.

Beyond that, the mother-daughter relationship that sometimes caused them both so much pain—but at other times drew them more closely together—remains an important and fascinating theme for research. Recent feminist studies of mother-daughter relationships have been inclined to emphasize conflict and tension, tending to blame the mother for the problem. Nancy Friday's *My Mother, My Self* exemplifies this approach. Linda Rosenzweig's recent study, *The Anchor of My Life: Middle-Class Mothers and Daughters, 1880-1920*, takes a more complex and nuanced approach to the subject and provides a useful model for further investigation of this subject. Anita Clair Fellman's 1990 article in *Signs*, "The Politics of a Mother-Daughter Relationship", is also full of penetrating insights on this topic.[13]

We also need to consider the nature of the marital relationship between Laura and Almanzo. This was much more obscure, in many ways, than the connection between mother and daughter and is one for which much less evidence is available.

Other questions invite continued discussion: what was the nature of Wilder's personality? What sort of person ultimately was she? Was she really a "prissy" little woman? Was she a "lovable" old lady? Was she a "spunky" girl who took after her father, in contrast to her sister Mary, who took after their mother? What were her motivations? What were her desires? What were her dreams and aspirations? How did she accommodate herself to reality? I address these issues, directly or indirectly, in my biography of Wilder but recognize that there is room for debate and for further evidence and argument.

When and how did Wilder learn how to write? If we agree that she was a capable novelist, what made her one? What was the process of training that went on?

What was her life like in Missouri? I devote the bulk of my book to the Missouri years. But what kinds of new facts can be uncovered, and what interpretive schemes might lead us to see Wilder in a new light?

Going back to her childhood and adolescence, we can ask the question that so many people are interested in: how did the books either differ from or conform to the actual lives lived by Laura and her family on the frontier?

Many themes present themselves for further contemplation. These include religion, memory, politics, community, social class, women's culture, agriculture, economics, the frontier, the landscape, the Great Plains, the Big Woods, the Midwest, the Ozarks, Missouri, and the American nation.

How much politics can be detected in the books? Was it put there by accident or design? What were Wilder's political views, and what were the influences molding them? How did they relate to or influence her daughter's views? Is there an inherent coincidence between frontier living and the Wilders' circumstances, on the one hand, and the conservative political views they all espoused, on the other? To what degree do readers of the books perceive an underlying conservative bias in the books, to what degree do they agree with them, and how much difference has it made in the popularity of the books?

Finally, the enduring popularity and appeal of the books remains a fascinating phenomenon. There are few American writers or historical figures who command the same sort of devotion and interest that Wilder does. People make pilgrimages to all of the historical sites associated with her. They read her books, not once or twice, but many times. Plausible explanations for her popularity can be suggested: the concrete, visual imagery contained in her books; her effective use of language; the simplicity of her moral vision; her emphasis on family values; nostalgia for frontier times; realization that these are basically true stories; and so forth. Still, the depth and continuity of Wilder's appeal remain elusive.

I will be interested to see what kind of press coverage this conference receives. I would guess that headlines and story leads will emphasize whatever is controversial or might involve a conflict. Recent examples of this tendency are the stories about a Wilder conference in Minneapolis dealing with Wilder's treatment of Native Americans, raising the question of whether she was an "Indian-hater," and reactions to the publication of William Holtz's biography of Rose Wilder Lane, which engendered headlines like "Little lie on the prairie?" and "'Little House' had no ghost, family friend says."[14]

I would like to suggest that Wilder's popularity as a novelist stems primarily from just the opposite tendency. It is not conflict, sensationalism, or controversy that most readers admire in her books which draws them back to read them over and over again. Rather, it is ordinariness, the commonplace, and the overwhelming factuality of everyday life that attracts them. Certainly problems, conflicts, and controversies play a role in her plots: wolves and panthers terrify little girls, blizzards threaten entire towns, greedy businessmen try to benefit from other people's miseries, and unruly schoolchildren make life unpleasant for their teachers. Wilder's books would be less interesting without the conflicts that arise between Laura and Mary, Eliza Jane Wilder, and Nellie Oleson or between Indians and settlers, homesteaders and thieving rascals, goldminers and government officials. But mostly we enjoy our recognition of the common, ordinary events of everyday life that Wilder treats in such loving detail and our ability to imagine ourselves among the characters that she describes.

It is this capacity to recreate the concreteness of people's lives and at the same time her casting these actions within the horizon of a recognizable moral perspective that keeps us returning to these books for pleasure and instruction

Endnotes

1. The question of authorship has been of interest since the Rose Wilder Lane Papers were opened and researchers began noting how Wilder's original, hand-written manuscripts were transformed in the process of editing into the final published versions of the books. Various book drafts and correspondence between Wilder and Lane document much of this process of collaboration. Rosa Ann Moore first demonstrated the significant role played by Lane in constructing her mother's books in "Laura Ingalls Wilder's Orange Notebooks and the Art of the Little House Books," *Children's Literature*, Vol. 4 (1975), 105-19; "The Little House Books: Rose-Colored Classics," *Ibid*. Vol. 7 (1978), 7-16; and "Laura Ingalls Wilder and Rose Wilder Lane: The Chemistry of Collaboration," *Children's Literature in Education II* (Autumn, 1980), 101-9. William T. Anderson dealt with the question much more extensively in "The Literary Apprenticeship of Laura Ingalls Wilder," *South Dakota History*, Vol. 13 (Winter, 1983), 285-331 and "Laura Ingalls Wilder and Rose Wilder Lane: The Continuing Collaboration," *Ibid*. Vol. 16 (Summer, 1986), 89-143. William Holtz took the issue to a new level in arguing that Lane actually ghosted her mother's books in *The Ghost in the Little House: A Life of Rose Wilder Lane* (Columbia: University of Missouri Press, 1993). The pendulum swung back toward granting Wilder more credit for the authoring of her own books in Caroline Fraser, "The Prairie Queen," *New York Review of Books*, Vol. 41 (December 22, 1994), 38-45; Ann Romines, *Constructing the Little House: Gender, Culture, and Laura Ingalls Wilder* (Amherst: University of Massachusetts Press, 1997); and John E. Miller, *Becoming Laura Ingalls Wilder: The Woman behind the Legend* (Columbia: University of Missouri Press, 1998).

2. Rose Wilder Lane, "I, Rose Wilder Lane . . . .," *Cosmopolitan*, Vol. 80 (June, 1926), 42; Lane, Journal entry, April 10, 1933, Diaries and Notes, 47, Rose Wilder Lane Papers, Herbert Hoover Presidential Library, West Branch, Iowa.

3. Laura Ingalls Wilder, *On the Way Home: The Diary of a Trip from South Dakota to Mansfield, Missouri, in 1894* (New York: Harper and Row, 1962).

4. Lionel Trilling, *The Liberal Imagination: Essays in Literature and Society* (New York: Viking, 1951), 211-12; Leon Edel, "The Subject Matter of Biography," in William H. Davenport and Ben Siegel, eds., *Biography Past and Present: Selections and Critical Essays* (New York: Charles Scribner's Sons, 1965), 117.

5. Doris Kearns Goodwin, "Angles of Vision," in Marc Pachter, ed., *Telling Lives: The Biographer's Art* (Philadelphia: University of Pennsylvania Press, 1985), 91.

6. Miller, *Becoming Laura Ingalls Wilder*, 11.

7. The notion that Wilder's progress toward authorship of the Little House series of novels involved a constant process of becoming a different person than she had been earlier is the central theme of my biography. The notion of "becoming" has been employed in a number of other studies, including Howard M. Feinstein, *Becoming William James* (Ithaca, N.Y.: Cornell University Press, 1984); Ormond Seavey, *Becoming Benjamin Franklin: The Autobiography and the Life* (Univer-

sity Park: Pennsylvania State University Press, 1988); Sarah Whitaker Peters, *Becoming O'Keeffe: The Early Years* (New York: Abbeville Press, 1991); and Emily Wortis Leider, *Becoming Mae West* (New York: Farrar Straus Giroux, 1997).

8. Copies of the *Missouri Ruralist* are available on microfilm. Many of Wilder's columns have been collected, in slightly edited form, in Stephen Hines, *Little House in the Ozarks: A Laura Ingalls Wilder Sampler: The Rediscovered Writings* (Nashville: Thomas Nelson, 1991). I discussed the themes and values incorporated in the columns in *Papers of the Twenty-Sixth Annual Dakota History Conference*, comp. Arthur R. Huseboe and Harry F. Thompson (Sioux Falls, South Dakota.: Augustana College, 1994), 481-88.

9. William Anderson, *A Little House Reader* (New York: HarperCollins, 1998), 119.

10. Holtz, *The Ghost in the Little House*, 380.

11. Miller, *Becoming Laura Ingalls Wilder*, 10.

12. Bart Kosko, *Fuzzy Thinking: The New Science of Fuzzy Logic* (New York: Hyperion, 1993).

13. Nancy Friday, *My Mother/My Self: The Daughter's Search for Identity* (New York: Delacorte, 1977); Linda Rosenzweig, *The Anchor of My Life: Middle-Class American Mothers and Daughters, 1880-1920* (New York: New York University Press, 1993); Anita Clair Fellman, "Laura Ingalls Wilder and Rose Wilder Lane: The Politics of a Mother-Daughter Relationship," *Signs: Journal of Woman in Culture and Society*, Vol. 15 (Spring, 1990), 535-61. Mother-daughter relationships are identified as one of several core topics by the editors of the recent collection, *The Challenge of Feminist Biography: Writing the Lives of Modern American Women*, ed. Sara Alpern, et al. (Urbana: University of Illinois Press, 1992), 5.

14. "'Little House' Books: Plums or Plum Wrong?" *Minneapolis Star-Tribune*, April 17, 1996, A1; John Berlau, "Little lie on the prairie?" *Columbia Missourian*, October 28, 1992; Cathy Karlin Zahner, "'Little House' had no ghost, family friend says," *Kansas City Star*, August 8, 1993.

The Frontier of the Little House

ANN ROMINES

It is November, 1952. In a few days it will be my tenth birthday. Today I am getting a special present, early. My grandmother has driven up from her house thirty miles away; soon we will get into her sturdy blue Chevrolet—just the two of us—and she will drive a hundred miles to the nearest city: Springfield, the Queen City of the Ozarks. Our destination is the Brown Bookstore, with its tall wood shelves and its air of seriousness and mystery. A famous author will be there today, signing books. My favorite author. Laura Ingalls Wilder.

That was a gray, cloudy November day with a threat of snow. My grandmother was not the world's best driver and my mother must have worried a bit as we set off on the curvy two-lane blacktop, in those days before seat belts and airbags. After fifty slow miles, just before the city limits of Mansfield, the road wound around a white farmhouse with a craggy gray rock chimney. That was Mrs. Wilder's house, we knew. My friend Rosanna and her family had stopped once to talk with Mrs. Wilder; they found her outside cracking black walnuts and glad to visit a while. But—although we prided ourselves on being neighborly in the Ozarks— my family was too reserved and I was too bashful to stop in her curving driveway on the way to Springfield. Today the farmhouse doors and windows were shut tight. Mr. Wilder, the Farmer Boy, was dead now and Mrs. Wilder (Laura!) was ahead of us on the highway, also speeding toward the magic space of the Brown Bookstore.

For several years, I had been competing with my gradeschool classmates for the well-worn copies of the Little House books on our county library's shelves. Once I had received a book of my own—*The Long Winter*—for a Christmas present. My third grade teacher had kept the whole class—even the boys! —in spellbound silence, reading *Little House on the Prairie* to us every day after lunch. My best girlfriends and I had acted out our favorite scenes from *On the Banks of Plum Creek* in the schoolyard, jeering at the victim who had to play Nellie Oleson, with leeches stuck to her legs, or prissy big sister Mary. We all wanted to be Laura, of course. I never got the part. (I was too tall.) But now I had read all the books except the last one, and I chattered to Grandmother about why I loved them so much, even more than *Little Women*.

I was dressed in my best and most grownup clothes; plaid pleated skirt and blue blazer. But when we entered the bookstore, I wanted to disappear. Who were all these OTHER little girls, pretty and hair bowed and chattering to each other in perky assurance? Except for Grandmother, no one spoke to me. I felt like Laura and Mary when they went to town to school and everyone stared and jeered, "Country girls!" and laughed at their dresses. Did Mrs. Wilder, my Author, belong to all these city girls I didn't know? (You can see them still, in the old newspaper photos of Laura Ingalls Wilder at her last booksigning, crowding around her and speaking right up.) Grandmother and I took our places in line. When our turn came, I didn't know what to say and stood tongue-tied and awkward, nobody's subject for a cute photograph. Mrs. Wilder was beautiful, with her white curls and dark red velvet dress (I had never seen a grownup in velvet in the daytime). Was *this* the brown-haired Laura of Plum Creek and De Smet?? With Grandmother's warm hand on my shaky shoulder, I stood and watched while Mrs. Wilder wrote—slowly, deliberately—on the first page of my new book. She wrote her name, Laura Ingalls Wilder.

I read that book, *These Happy Golden Years*, in the warm car on the long ride home, rushing greedily to cover as many pages as possible before the early November dark fell—even though I knew that, when I finished, there would be no more new Little House stories for me to read. I still have the book. And I still have the unforgettable day my grandmother gave me, with all its buzz of unspeakable questions.

I've been telling you a story about a frontier experience. It's not the story a historian would be likely to tell—and today I'm surrounded by distinguished historians, who can probably tell the *history* of "Laura Ingalls Wilder and the American Frontier" more authoritatively than I, making the proper stops at Frederick Jackson Turner and elsewhere. I've been thinking, however, about the revisionist version of "frontier" proposed recently by literary and cultural critic Annette Kolodny. Today, Kolodny urges, we should recognize the "frontier" as a locus of first cultural contact, circumscribed by a particular physical terrain in the process of change *because* of the forms that contact takes, all of it inscribed by the collisions and interpenetrations of language. . . . [This is experienced by] a currently indigenous population and at least one group of newcomer 'intruders.'[1]

In my recent book,[2] I write about how complexly the Little House series explores this fresh concept of frontier, as the Ingallses have their first contacts with persons whose languages—Osage, French, Norwegian—they do not speak and whose cultures they cannot fully comprehend. Often the Ingallses are the newcomer intruders that Kolodny describes, in an environment that is being transformed by their presence and their priorities, as they break sod, plant wheat, kill animals, build big railroads and little houses.

Today, I'd like to suggest that we also look at the Brown Bookstore (and all the others like it) as a frontier environment. When I walked through that door, I had my first conscious experience of a "culture of letters" that extended beyond me and my classmates and family and teachers and librarian, who all knew me by name. My Author and her texts were suddenly a contested territory—here were stacks of glossy books that anyone could buy, and other girls who wore fashionable clothes and addressed my Author in easy, practiced language that I could not speak. Newly arrived from the country of my own rapt, self-absorbed reading, I had crossed the borders of a literary marketplace where the Little House was becoming a major cultural phenomenon of the twentieth century United States. Perhaps my own life as a teacher and scholar of American women's writing and cultures began on that day. For, on that frontier, I saw that being an Author (who had been a girl) was more complicated than I'd known. To think and talk about all that I'd seen, I dimly realized I was going to need new language.

When I first encountered the Little House books in the 1950s, they had already been embraced by enthusiastic American readers for twenty years. Their account of the exigencies of the nineteenth-century frontier had struck responsive chords in a stressed Depression market, and later, in the fifties, they reinforced a postwar emphasis on family and domestic values—while garnering most of the major honors for U.S. children's literature. When my Girl Scout troop dramatized scenes from "classic" children's books in an elementary school "Book Friends" pageant, Laura and Mary Ingalls were the hands-down favorite characters among the children, although the Little House books were—by decades—the *newest* classics in the program, among *Tom Sawyer, Pinocchio, Alice in Wonderland,* and *Little Women.*

A few months after my trip to the Brown Bookstore, the new Little House edition appeared on the market to immediate success; the art-deco-inflected illustrations of *my* Little House books were replaced by the drawings of Garth Williams, already a huge success with mass-market Little Golden Books. And today, as any visitor to the children's section of a bookstore knows, Little House titles still occupy a sizeable and contested strip of shelf space, joined by a growing array of books, spin-offs and products. The Little House logo, proud property of HarperCollins, has the same kind of widespread name recognition as Kleenex or the Nike swoosh, making it one of the major, enduring market successes of the twentieth century.

As I grew up in the Missouri Ozarks, Wilder's chosen home for more than sixty years, I could see that transformation happening. As the children's paperback market expanded, more kids had the entire set of mass-marketed Little House books in their proprietary box, instead of the worn library copies my friends and I had vied for. And, soon after Mrs. Wilder's death in 1957, her house became a place I no longer had to be too shy to visit—paying my admission fee gave me full rights to the full tour, from Mrs. Wilder's kitchen sink and writing desk to Mr. Wilder's carpentry to the books and mail-order catalogs on their tables and shelves. In the first month the house was open, my family made the trip, and Mr. and Mrs. Lichty, the Wilders' friends and the first curators of the house, showed us around themselves; we were their only customers. Already there were things to buy, and we came home with a musty 1933 copy of Rose Wilder Lane's *Let the Hurricane Roar* (in which I hoped to discover a Little House sequel, but was disappointed) and—for me, although I was too old for dolls—a replica of Laura's rag doll, Charlotte, handstitched by a local Mansfield woman. As I grew up and went off to college (Charlotte went with me), to graduate school, and to jobs, I never tired of annual returns to the Wilder house in Mansfield. Every year there seemed to be a new attraction—Pa's fiddle returned from South Dakota, the new museum with Rose Wilder Lane's possessions after her death, Ma Ingalls' crocheting and Mary's quilting, the ever-expanding bookstore and gift shop, which I can remember in a half a dozen different locations, each bigger (and more enticing) than the last. Never again did my family or friends and I find ourselves the only customers—the parking lot (which has also expanded repeatedly) was now jammed with vans and cars from all over North America, and sometimes one could hear languages that clearly were not English. One thing I noticed, more and more—although my fellow pilgrims included lots of children, often the most ardent were adults like me, especially women. In the museum, we crowded intently close to the glass cases, calling out to our children or companions, "Look! Mary's nine-patch! Laura's bread plate! Ma's gold pen shaped like a feather!"

In my adult life, propelled by the passion for reading that had been nurtured by the Little House books, I had become a college English professor, a scholar who wrote about American women's writing and culture. Such an object as Caroline Quiner Ingalls' pearl-handled pen shaped like a feather should have meant a great deal to me, as signifier of a tradition of women's writing that looked back to the quill pen and forward to the telegraph and typewriter employed by Rose Wilder Lane, a tradition of private and public writing that was passed from mother to daughter and back again, in the Quiner-Ingalls-Wilder family. But I didn't get it. Laura Ingalls Wilder's books remained a part of my life as a rapt and adoring fan, untouched by the kinds of critical reading and thinking I was doing in my professional life.

None of this changed until about ten years ago, when I was in Red Cloud, Nebraska, attending a seminar on Willa Cather, one of the authors I write about regularly. Immersed in that prairie landscape, thinking about how it helped to shape Cather's career—one of the great careers of the twentieth century—I suddenly found that I couldn't stop thinking about another great career—that of Laura Ingalls Wilder. I began to buttonhole my startled fellow seminar participants for Little House conversations, and I was surprised to find that many of them found this subject as intense, as freighted, and as central to their personal histories as I did. Dimly, I began to realize that the Little House was also a great subject for scholars, and I went home eager to find and read all the scholarship I knew must be out there.

I found a great deal—work on biography and place and child readers, histories with clues that led me to other writings by Wilder and introduced me to the previously unthinkable proposition that Rose Wilder Lane was her mother's co-author. Through a few published quotations, I became aware of tantalizing Wilder-Lane letters and other unpublished papers that made me itch to get to the Hoover Library and other archives. But when I looked for work that analyzed the Little House books as a literary/cultural construct and achievement, I struck out. When I'd looked for such work on Willa Cather, who was Wilder's contemporary and also had a wide—but no wider!—readership, I had hit pay dirt, coming up with hundreds of articles and dozens of books. But with Wilder the case was different: I came up with just a dozen or so articles, scattered over a span

of twenty years. In my other work on American women writers, I'd been
supported by all the growing resources of feminist scholarship, which had
helped us to discover a wide range of women's texts and pioneered new
ways of reading them and their histories. The new climate of cultural studies, in which barriers between "literary" and "popular" texts were dissolving
and "children's literature" was no longer ghettoized as a separate and lesser
enterprise, was supportive too. Suddenly, and elatedly, I realized that the
Little House books, my first favorites, were also and still a *frontier* for a
literary critic. And so I found myself trying to become a settler in this new
territory—a territory already inhabited by other readers with other priorities. Some of those readers, in fact, were my own former selves.

For I found that for me, and for many other Americans, the Little
House series itself was a liminal—borderland—territory. These books are
often read and reread over the course of a lifetime (for the very first children
who read the series are now entering their seventies). Adults may bring a
long history of reading experiences to their current encounters with the books,
and often they find their different selves are at odds. For example, when my
feminist-scholar-self approached this frontier, pen in hand and ready to dis-
sect the patriarchal constructs in Wilder and Lane's books, she was met by
my indignant nine-year-old fan/self, deep in the throes of her own family
romance and unwilling to hear a single critical word about Pa Ingalls. The
women's literary historian, eager to explore the working of perhaps the only
documented mother-daughter collaboration among canonical American authors, met the loyalist of Brown Bookstore, insistent that Laura, her Author, had written every single word all by herself. And the cultural historian
tangled with the chronicler of personal history, for the Little House had long
been entwined with the most intimate stuff of my own life. At one point,
when I tried to write about the history of dolls as an ambivalent force for
socializing young girls as it is evoked in the Little House series, my own
long-cherished Charlotte seemed to object, her black button eyes snapping
in protest. All these antagonists seemed to circle my desk as I tried to write,
and the jangle of their voices was like the cacophony of contesting voices
that Kolodny describes on a frontier.

As I wrote, I had to try to accommodate all these "I"s and to find
places and ways for them to speak in my book. For I believe that the Little
House books have performed some of the best functions of frontier culture for American readers of the past decades, providing a site where we
can meet to explore deeply felt issues at the centers of our lives and our
histories, with the Little House as a central figure in all our various languages, although we may pronounce it and construe it differently.

Each of the five chapters of my book, then, has one of these issues at its center. I began at the beginning, with a fact that has always puzzled me: Wilder's statement that she began writing her books in order to preserve her father's stories, which were "too good to be lost."[3] This disturbed me because I'd always seen the first value of the Little House series in its girl protagonist and its steadfast commitment to giving full weight and primary attention to the unfolding story of a girl's life and sensibility. Going back to *Little House in the Big Woods*, I realized why this had always been my least favorite of the books about Laura. The centerpiece of this book is the stories Pa tells to his rapt daughters. I had never much liked those stories. They are classic tales of male initiation, teaching men and boys the conditions of physical and psychic survival in the natural world. But none of the stories contains a single female figure, and they all take place in the woods, where Laura and Mary are never allowed to go. Ma teaches her daughters various domestic skills, but she tells no stories. The excitement and invention of storytelling (which would become Wilder's and Lane's life work) and the confirming importance of being a protagonist seem reserved for males. As I look again, I can see that the narrative also has subtle moments of testing these disturbing patriarchal principles. On Christmas, Laura's aunt and uncle vie with each other to tell the story of Aunt Eliza's near-encounter with a predatory panther; although the story happened to Aunt Eliza, Uncle Peter seems to assume that it is his to tell. At the sugaring-off dance, Laura watches in amazement and delight as her Grandma Ingalls defeats her spry young son in a jigging contest. But Grandma has no chance to bask in her moment as heroine; immediately she must run to the kitchen to dish out the boiling maple syrup, or the valuable batch will be wasted. Once Laura snatches her own moment as heroine when, in a playfully seductive game, Pa plays the part of "Mad Dog" and pursues his little daughters around the room in a frenzied chase. Instead of cowering, like Mary, Laura takes a "wild leap... over the woodbox, dragging Mary with her" and wins the game: all "at once there was no mad dog at all. There was only Pa standing there with his blue eyes shining, looking at Laura."[4] For a moment, the little girl has put herself at the center of the story. But at the book's end, the child is drowsy and compliant, listening to the soporific sound of her father's voice in an eternal present. "Now is now," she thinks. "It can never be a long time ago."[5] In some ways, this first Little House book, seems a near-total victory for patriarchal control.

And then—to my childhood chagrin—the next Little House book bluntly announces in its title that it is not about Laura at all but about a *boy*—Farmer Boy Almanzo Wilder. This second book is based on Rose Wilder Lane's father's stories. Almanzo is clearly an active protagonist in his book, as Laura usually is not, and the book ends with the boy's choice of profession, continuing in his father's patriarchal footsteps as a farmer. *Farmer Boy*, I must admit, was the only Little House book I never returned to reread in my childhood; once, I concluded, was *more* than enough.

These two first books were written and published in the worst years of the Great Depression. As Barbara Melosh has written, in these years "the strains of economic depression reinforced the containment of feminism. . . . As men lost their jobs, wage-earning women [as both Wilder and Lane had been] became the targets of public hostility and restrictive policy. One slogan exhorted, 'Don't take a job from a man!'"[6] Lane, especially, was thinking of her mother's novels as a way to insure her aging parents' financial security, for the men of the family —Charles Ingalls, Almanzo Wilder, and his father James Wilder—had all failed to provide their families with enduring financial security through their work as farmers. Lane had been the financial hero of her family's story—and now she was beginning to put her mother in that central position, as well. By writing and publishing for a mass audience, these women—who both loved their fathers and conceived of themselves as conventionally dutiful daughters—had preempted the patriarchal spotlight, and had done so in ways that might make them vulnerable to censure in the conservative Depression climate. The male emphasis and acts of male homage in the first two books reflect this complex situation and the uncertainties of two woman authors caught in the first stages of an amorphous collaboration. With Laura dozing in unchanging domestic routine at the end of *Little House in the Big Woods* and Almanzo the uncontested hero of *Farmer Boy*—and a publisher who paid less for the second book than for the first—where could the Little House story go?

The simple answer to that question, of course, was WEST— toward the historic nineteenth-century American frontier. The dreamlike intensity and historical urgency of the beautiful third book, *Little House on the Prairie*, are made possible when the Ingalls family hit the road, as emigrants to Kansas Indian Territory. Now the Little House has become a *serial*, not a static locale, and it offers possibilities of continuation and growth that give Laura, as a frontier girl protagonist, space to run and think and imagine and grow. The central issue initiated by this book is the collision of cultures that is a classic component of frontier experience, the "first cultural contact" that Kolodny describes. Although the Ingallses are squatters on Osage land, they set up a homestead in classic northern European American style, with cultivated fields, a wooden house and indoor domestic routines. But they find that their Indian neighbors have very different ways of inhabiting the prairie, with a migratory life style, outdoor cooking, and the annual custom of burning off the land (thus endangering the Ingalls house and crops). Ma's policy about these neighbors is very simple: "Let Indians keep to themselves," she says, "and we will do the same"[7]. Pa is more receptive and more curious, but he also remains entirely committed to his own priorities: he has come to Kansas Indian Territory to be a successful "white settler," claiming the "best land" for his farm with the aim of prospering and living "like a king." It is the central, exploratory consciousness of the child Laura that makes it possible to raise complex and crucial issues of acculturation in this book. Laura's most eager desire in coming to Indian Territory has been "to see a papoose" and thus to see another way of being an American child, outside the Ingalls family and the Little House.

Laura's new vision produces some of the richest scenes in the entire series and, I would argue, in twentieth century American writing. Exploring an Indian camp with Pa, she and Mary are taught to read the smallest signs of the Osage women's domestic routines, almost like young ethnologists, nineteenth-century style, but their attention is deflected by bright trade beads in the dust, and they greedily gather up these "artifacts," abandoned Indian property, and squabble about what to do with them. When Indian men enter the Ingalls' house while Pa is away and direct Ma to cook for them, Laura is torn between her fear of what the men may do to Ma and her curiosity about these compelling strangers, who speak a language she does not understand but (like Pa) demand to be fed by her mother. Laura's ambivalence about how to see the Indian men is brilliantly suggested when she hides behind a plank leaning against the wall of the house but cannot resist peering out to take in every detail of the men's clothing, bodies, demeanor, and smell. When she takes the risk of seeing, of course, the men look back at her, and the little girl ducks back into her retreat. The simple device of the plank expresses Laura's warring fear and desire to see and comprehend Indians, as well as all the structural impediments that her culture offers to such vision. And it conveys the extraordinary stresses and tensions that burdened even the simplest contact between European American females and Indian men.

Laura's desire to see an Indian child is finally fulfilled as the family witnesses the hieratic departure of the Osage after their war council. Riding "gay little ponies," Osage children are blissfully naked, and Laura has "a naughty wish to be a little Indian girl,"[8] although she knows this is

naughty and an inadmissible desire, something she must not "really mean."
Laura's sense of the possible has been richly expanded by her glimpses of
Indian cultures, and this produces a sudden utterance that is perhaps her
most startling and audacious in the series. "'Pa,' she said, 'get me that
little Indian baby!'" Ma objects,

> "Why on earth do you want an Indian baby, of all things! . . .
> "Its eyes are so black," Laura sobbed. She could not say what she meant.
> "Why Laura," Ma said, "You don't want another baby. We have a baby,
> our own baby."
> "I want the other one, too!" Laura sobbed, loudly.[9]

This passionate cry gives voice to the most piercing tensions of
frontier settlement *and* of the multi-cultural possibilities of American life.
While Laura's demand for the baby may express a sense of cultural entitle-
ment that views the Indian child as an *object* of desire, the intense look she
exchanges with the baby also suggests that she is trying to broach possibilities of a shared lifestyle and a shared life between the European American and Native American children. However futilely, she is reaching toward an extended family that she might share with both her white sisters
and an Indian baby. Laura's upbringing offers no way to express such a
wish; "she could not say what she meant." But her unseemly outburst is a
female child's explosive critique of the languages offered by her own culture; it voices her yearning for a life of expansion, inclusion and acculturation that she has begun to intuit in Kansas.

Such scenes, I argue, make the Little House series a far more
complex cultural frontier than we critics have yet acknowledged. In the
newly mobile Laura, Wilder and Lane found a sensibility that could begin
to express the accelerating desires and pressures of a borderland girlhood.
The tensions of this book's rendering of Indian issues have made *Little
House on the Prairie* currently the most controversial of the Little House
books.[10] What we don't note so frequently is the fact that issues of acculturation continued to be evoked in the later Little House books, although
they became a more and more muted subtext, suppressed as Laura approached sexual maturity and—as a young schoolteacher—became a
spokesperson for her community of white settlers. Consider the Norwegian neighbors on Plum Creek, for example—or Big Jerry, the half-breed
and possible outlaw who is Laura's first crush (although she never speaks
a word to him). Or the thrilling climax of the literary entertainment in De
Smet: an amateur minstrel show in which the white men of the town,

including Pa Ingalls, enjoy a chance to slip out of the constraints of their patriarchal and racial identities, for at least one night.[11] Such a scene is both liberating and horrifying—and by now, the teenage Laura is firmly placed not on the stage, but in the audience. Compared to the great possibilities of Kansas territory, where Indian cultures had variety and dignity and a black doctor was a valued and respected citizen, the minstrel show offers solidarity and release to whites through a debased parody of African American culture, and it tells a white girl that her frontier is now diminished, so that she cannot—even for a moment—escape from her white skin and her white female position.

One of the most persistent features of my own relation to the Little House story has been an attachment to the *things* in the Little House. Like other fans, I crowd the museums to see the objects that Wilder and Lane evoked with such intensity, poring over Laura's china jewel box and cardboard name cards, and longing—always!—to catch a glimpse of Ma's china shepherdess. Remember the intensity that commodities provoke in these books! Pa's eyes shine with emotion as he delivers his purchases of window glass, a cast iron stove, a sewing machine. And who can forget Nellie Olesen's wax doll, Laura's Christmas furs, or Mary's best dress? Another of my chapters is built around the romance of the market and all its complex meanings for American girls (meanings that continue to proliferate as rapidly as the Little House products do). The romance of buying is another of the reasons we keep reading these books.

According to Walter Benn Michaels, a "fundamentally critical" attitude toward "consumer capitalism" has characterized most of "the most powerful works of American culture".[12] Another striking and valuable feature of the Little House books is that they express a more complex and ambivalent attitude toward consumer capitalism. In *On the Banks of Plum Creek*, for example, Laura enters an intense consumer rivalry with a storekeeper's daughter, Nellie Oleson, and Nellie's weapons in that rivalry are always commodities, like the opulent doll that Laura may not touch. Although Nellie may imply excesses of consumption, the Ingalls girls get their own education in the importance of buying in this book: they delight in all the features of Ma's brand new stove, right down to its patent number. They make their first independent purchase, splitting a Christmas penny to buy a slate pencil from their preferred storekeeper (not Nellie's father!). Ma makes a rare shopping expedition to buy fabric for new dresses into an important lesson. First she asks, "What do you think of this golden-brown flannel, Laura?" Then,

Ma laid some narrow red braid across the golden brown, saying, "I think three
rows of this braid.... What do you think, Laura? Would that be pretty?"
"Oh yes, Ma!" Laura said. She looked up, and her eyes and Pa's bright
blue eyes danced together.
"Get it, Caroline," said Pa. . . .
Then Mary must have a new dress, but she did not like anything there.
So they all crossed the street to Mr. Oleson's store. There they found
dark blue flannel and narrow gilt braid, which was just what Mary
wanted.[13]

As the Ingalls girls come of age in the last decades of the nineteenth century, modern consumer culture (featuring catalogs and credit,
among other things) is just beginning to flourish, and middle class women
are coming into their own as key consumers. Here, combining fabrics and
trimmings with their mother's guidance, these girls are learning to use the
marketplace as a scene of aesthetic decisions, as they begin to package
themselves in clothes they have helped to design. Mary also learns to
survey the range of choices in more than one store and to participate in the
dynamics of supply and demand by her discriminating choice. And the
buying perpetuates the romance between Laura and her father; the intense
look that passes between them confirms that they both delight in Pa's
purchasing power, which can fulfill Laura's desires.

Later, Laura will begin to spend her own first earnings, and she
and Ma will pour their earnings and their labor into an incredibly elaborate
dress for Mary to wear to college, a dress so heavy and so freighted with
significance that Mary almost faints when she puts it on. But a major
triumph of Mary's college education will be that it teaches her to buy
again, making intelligent, discriminating choices as a thoughtful consumer,
instead of a blind mannequin. One of the great and mostly unacknowl-
edged appeals of the Little House books, especially for young readers, is
that they frankly acknowledge what all children know: that buying occa-
sions, like Laura's ecstatic moments choosing her new dress, are not trivial.
Instead, these books take seriously the shopping decisions by which most
of us work out the relation between our cultures' prescriptions about what
we *must* buy and our sense of self-determination and individual expres-
sion. The marketplace is another of the Little House frontiers.

When I was discovering the Wilder-Lane correspondence in the
Hoover Library archives, one letter in particular riveted my attention. In
1938, Wilder wrote to Lane about her struggles with the manuscript of
The Long Winter:

Here is what is bothering me and holding me up. I can't seem to find a plot, or pattern as you call it. There seems to be nothing to it only the struggle to live, through the winter. . . . This of course they all did. But is it strong enough . . . to supply the necessary thread running all through the book.

I could make a book with the plot being Laura's struggles to be, and success in becoming a teacher. . . .That would be a plot. . . . But it seems to weaken it. To be a sort of anti-climax. . . . I don't like it. But where is the plot in Hard Winter?[14]

This letter fascinated me, first, because it is so clearly the outburst of a committed writer wrestling with the exigencies of her craft—a writer who is addressing a trusted collaborator whom she clearly regards as an equal: no more, no less. And second, I was interested in the timing of the letter. *The Long Winter* is the fifth Little House book about the Ingalls family; why are these questions about plot only surfacing now?

The answer, I think, is that *The Long Winter* is the first of the books that is not shaped, overtly, by a project initiated by Pa: going West to Kansas, building a farm in Minnesota, working for the railroad and establishing a claim in Dakota. Now, in the grip of seven months of blizzard, there is nowhere for Pa to go, no plot for him to complete; only the most basic acts of maintenance: feeding the stock, twisting hay for the fire. Ma's work, of course, has always been basic acts of maintenance: cooking, sewing, cleaning, laundry, household invention. It is her skills that get the family through the winter; with Laura's help, she figures out how to prepare food, make a light, and sustain her children when the family and the town's resources are almost entirely gone. In *The Long Winter*, Wilder and Lane at last decided to foreground the world of Caroline Ingalls and her daughters, waiting in one room in confined intimacy and anxiety knowing only fragments of the male stories taking place outside the Little House. Conventional plots end with triumphs of will and resolution—but in *The Long Winter* the goal is simply the circular tasks of housekeeping, staying alive today and then starting the same round again, tomorrow. In her letter, Wilder is confronting matters that Rachel Blau du Plessis says faced most twentieth-century women who tried to write fiction: "What stories can be told? How can plots be resolved? What is felt to be narratable by both literary and social conventions?"[15] The story of women's day-to-day work of domestic survival has usually *not* been thought to be narratable, at best, it has been indicated as a background for the more flamboyantly dramatic stuff of male plots—just as, in *Little House in*

the Big Woods, little Laura enjoyed buttermaking and breadbaking with
her mother, but concluded that "the best time of all was at night, when Pa
came home" to tell his exciting male stories.[16] But, in *The Long Winter*, it
is Ma who is the resourceful hero; the book celebrates her saving skills
and her endurance. The *Long Winter* was the Little House book I reread
most often as a child, and I've been amazed by the number of girls and
women who've told me that it is their favorite Little House book.

In the last two Little House books, Wilder and Lane finally faced
the problem of finding plots that would express the full possibilities of
their rich portrait of a girl who is becoming a young woman. They
managed this by giving the last two books multiple plots, enacted by
women. Although courtship is the most conventional and common of
plots for nineteenth-century female protagonists, Laura and Almanzo
Wilder's courtship is *not* the single dominant pattern of these books,
although they began by thinking it would be: it is interwoven with the
engrossing story of Laura's apprenticeship as a schoolteacher—which
includes her terrifying confinement with Mrs. Brewster. Also part of
this complex pattern is Laura's deepening relationship with her mother
and the subtle beginnings of her life as a woman writer. These interre-
lated fictional plots resemble those of Wilder and Lane's own lives, and
they also mirror the pattern of multiple, simultaneous plots that has
marked the lives of most American women. In fact, the plotting of the
next-to-last book, *Little Town on the Prairie*, is set in motion by Laura's
first paying job. And by the time the series is complete, the various ways
that its various women characters earn money constitute a near-compre-
hensive survey of the major paid and unpaid occupations of rural women
in the nineteenth-century U.S.—buttermaking, taking boarders, sewing,
hatmaking, claimsitting, teaching, housekeeping, gardening, raising chick-
ens. In the Depression years when these books were written, they opened
up new territory by bringing woman's labor to the center of the written
page, through the Little House plots.

As I said at the beginning, in my memories of my long-ago day at
the Brown Bookstore, I am tongue-tied, struck silent in awe. But my
mother tells the story differently, as she heard it from Grandmother. According to her, I did say something: like so many other children, I asked
Mrs. Wilder if she were going to write any more books. And Mrs. Wilder
said, NO. It was that statement that I couldn't bear to remember. To end
the Little House series, I thought, would be like closing the frontier, shut-
ting down a whole era of expansion and possibility, where a girl could be
the center of a rich, engrossing story, and then grow up to write that story

herself. If the Little House frontier were closed, what could become of a girl like me? I agreed with Marjorie Vitense, a little girl who wrote Mrs. Wilder a fan letter from Iowa in 1933, after reading *Little House in the Big Woods*. Marjorie said, "I wish it would never come to an end for it was so good".[17]

Thus, one of the most exciting discoveries of my adult life has been what I have described: the realization that the Little House series is *still* a frontier territory. In these eight books, Wilder and Lane created a space where girls and boys, children and adults, historians, biographers, and literary/cultural scholars, with all our various languages, can come together to discuss some of the most difficult, intimate, and important questions of our lives.

End Notes

1. Annette Kolodny, "Letting Go Our Grand Obsessions: Notes Toward a New Literary History of the American Frontiers." *American Literature*, 64 (March 1992), 3, 5.

2. Ann Romines, *Constructing the Little House: Gender, Culture, and Laura Ingalls Wilder*. (Amherst, University of Massachusetts Press, 1997).

3. Laura Ingalls Wilder, "Laura's Book Fair Speech." *A Little House Sampler*, ed. William T. Anderson, (Lincoln University of Nebraska Press, 1988) 217.

4. Wilder, *Little House in the Big Woods*, 1932, (New York, Harper and Row, 1953) 36.

5. Ibid. 238.

6. Barbara Melosh. *Engendering Culture: Manhood and Womanhood in New Deal Public Art and Theater*. (Washington, D.C., Smithsonian Institution Press, 1991) 1.

7. Ibid., 309-10.

8. Ibid., 307.

9. Ibid., 309-10.

10. Michael Dorris. "Trusting the Words." *Booklist* 1-15, (June 1993) 1820-22; and Dennis McAuliffe, *The Deaths of Sibyl Bolton* (New York: Times Books, 1994).

11. In this discussion of the cultural functions of minstrel shows, I have been influenced by both of the following works: Erick Lott, *Love and Theft: Blackface Minstrelsy and the American Working Class*, (New York, Oxford University Press, 1993); and Robert C. Toll, *Blacking Up: The Minstrel Show in Nineteenth-Century America*, (New York, Oxford University Press, 1974).

12. Walter Benn Michaels, *The Gold Standard and the Logic of Naturalism*, (Berkeley, University of California Press, 1987) 14-15.

13. Wilder, *On The Banks of Plum Creek*, 1937, (New York, Harper and Row, 1953), 242.

14. Laura Ingalls Wilder to Rose Wilder Lane, February 19, 1938, Correspondence, Laura Ingalls Wilder Series, Rose Wilder Lane Papers, Herbert Hoover Presidential Library.

15. Rachel Blau du Plessis, *Writing Beyond the Ending: Narrative Strategies of Twentieth-Century Women Writers*, (Washington, DC, Smithsonian Institution Press, 1985), 3.

16. Wilder, *Little House in the Big Woods*, 1932, (New York, Harper and Row, 1953), 33.

17. Marjorie Vitense to Laura Ingalls Wilder, February 22, 1933, Western Historical Collection, University of Missouri-Columbia.

The Little House Books in
American Culture

ANITA CLAIR FELLMAN

These days Americans encounter Laura Ingalls Wilder and the Little House books not just as children, but throughout their lives. Parents read the books to their offspring who also meet "Laura Ingalls Wilder" in nineteenth-century dress at their local public library telling them about her life. Elementary school teachers read the books aloud to children or teach them to read by means of excerpts reprinted in basal readers. Countless classroom social studies activities are based on the books. Wilder is a common choice when students take on the identity of famous persons, the better to study them. On field trips with their class or on outings with their families to museums, pioneer villages, and interpretive centers, children again encounter Wilder who often stands in for the entire pioneer experience. Members of Little House reading clubs compete for opportunities to visit "the little town on the prairie," and Girl Scouts are able to work for a Laura Ingalls Wilder badge.

As adults, Americans open newspapers and magazines, ranging from *The Washington Post* to the *Orange County Register*, from *American Heritage* to *Diversion Travel Planner* or the *University of Chicago Alumni Magazine* and find articles about, or references to, Wilder and the Little House series. Scanning the *New York Times Book Review* list in 1996 of the 100 most notable books published in the first century of that magazine's existence, readers saw *Little House in the Big Woods* highlighted as the selection for 1932. Fans of "Prairie Home Companion" on National Public Radio periodically hear Garrison Keillor weave Wilder or her books into his monologue or one of the sketches on the program. Web surfers can encounter her on the Internet. The books themselves (not to mention the recent spin-off calendars, diaries, songbook, paper dolls, etc.) are to be found in virtually every bookstore as well as in buying clubs like Costco or Sam's. Even if they are not among the tens of thousands of fans annually who travel to various sites where the Ingalls and Wilder families lived, children and adults may find themselves driving on the Laura Ingalls Wilder Historic Highway in the upper Midwest. Tired of yet another production of "A Christmas Carol," they may choose instead to attend a new musical, "A Little House Christmas," which has become an annual holiday event in some cities. Whether they attend a history and literature club meeting in Kansas or a mother and daughter supper at their church in Michigan, an American Association of Retired People meeting in Wyoming or are resident in a retirement home in South Dakota or Nebraska, adults may encounter a presentation on Wilder or a reading from one of the Little House books.

Why am I interested in all these seemingly unrelated, perhaps trivial details about the books? Since there is something about the Little House books that brings out the storyteller in everyone, I too have a tale to tell about how I came to turn my scholarly attention to Wilder and her books and why I am preoccupied with Little House sightings in American culture. I cannot claim, like Ann Romines or William T. Anderson, to have been a devoted fan in childhood although I read the books as I worked my way semi-methodically through the children's room of the Blackstone Public Library in Chicago. As an adult my recollections of the books were vague—I remembered Almanzo's horses best I think. Nonetheless, I must have had positive associations with them, for when the time came in the 1970's to choose books to read to my own small children, the Wilder books were among those holdovers from my childhood that I was determined to foist upon them. Indeed, the Little House books were the first chapter books that I read in turn to my two sons. It wasn't until the second marathon reading session, five years after the first, that a series of epiphanies occurred to me that drew me into a project that is now of very long duration.

At the time of the second reading, our family was residing in a suburb of Vancouver, British Columbia, which is the western edge of quite another frontier. Our house was perched on the side of a steep hill. The pitch of our yard, plus its popularity with those enormous slugs peculiar to the Pacific coast, dictated that we grow nothing except grass and some hardy marigolds. By background and inclination we were an urban family. Nonetheless, after I had finished reading *Little House in the Big Woods*, that depiction of a Protestant Garden of Eden in which everything the

Ingalls family needs is available through the bounty of the land and woods and the labor of their own hands, my younger son turned to me with shining eyes and asked earnestly, "Oh, Mom, can we live that?" I was taken aback. "Wow," I thought to myself, "that is a powerful fantasy indeed." And then a funny thing happened as I read the series aloud this second time: I found myself reluctant to have the books come to an end. Instead of reading three chapters a night, I cut the allotment first to two and then to one. And I reduced my pace. As I was slowly enunciating the last pages of the last chapters, I was struggling to keep the tears out of my voice. "There is something going on here!" I thought. "I wonder what the hook is; why have I become so captivated by these books?"

From that point a series of serendipitous occurrences and coincidences served to push me into this project. Around 1980, I accidentally discovered, by glancing at a book entitled *The Discovery of Freedom* that had been left on a table in my university library, that Laura's daughter, Rose, was a libertarian thinker. "How interesting," I thought. "I wonder if that means that Laura was a libertarian too. And what would that suggest about the Little House books?" And then a librarian mentioned to me that she had seen an article by someone named Rosa Anne Moore indicating that the Little House books were the product of a collaboration between Laura and Rose. That information made me wonder all the more about the nature of the influences between mother and daughter. If Rose was a libertarian and Laura and Rose worked together on the books, then did any of Rose's ideas find their way into the books? My first trip to the Hoover Presidential Library in 1983 was to examine the women's papers for indications of intellectual exchange between them. It was then that I discovered their highly charged emotional relationship and began to wonder about the connection between people's emotional lives and their intellectual and ideological positions.

Like many a good story, mine has a moral, or at least a message, to it. You can see by this recapitulation of my entry into this project, that like most other scholars, I undertake a particular bit of research out of a combination of passion, intellectual curiosity, and accident. But of course, I wasn't then and am not now living in a historical vacuum. What I chose as compelling about the books and the authors' lives had a lot to do with the era in which I was living. As I was beginning to think about this project, Ronald Reagan was elected President. During that first election campaign, I was very much struck by the individualist, anti-government nature of his rhetoric, his insistence that individuals were essentially responsible for themselves and that government was not needed, or wanted, to protect them from the fluctuations of the market or other misfortunes. We have become accustomed to such ideas and language now, but in 1980, it had been a long time since such language was used so fulsomely and frequently in the political arena. Because the New Deal had changed the nature of American political discourse, the language of conservatism, from the 1930's until Reagan, was more overly traditionalist and anti-Communist than it was anti-government.[1]

Whatever I thought of the match between Reagan's rhetoric and the actuality of most Americans' daily lives in the complex economy and society of 1980, I was deeply impressed by the evident responsiveness of Americans to his vision. It was as if Reagan had siphoned a stream of laissez faireism that ran forcefully and persistently just under the surface of American life.[2] What fed that stream, I wondered? What kept such ideas alive? What gave them such emotional force? Slowly I began to consider the possibility that in the absence of a consistently articulated individualist perspective in mainstream politics, other sources, perhaps especially in popular culture, were responsible for maintaining this vision.

As I read and reread the Little House books in the light of the Lane/Wilder papers and the responses to the books by critics and other readers, several things became clear to me. One was that the collaboration between Wilder and Lane, occurring during the New Deal which both opposed, heightened the stress on individual and familial self-sufficiency in the books. As the two women pondered how to tell the Ingalls family story, they gravitated toward framing incidents in ways that emphasized the isolation of the family and the strictly voluntary nature of its association with others. I also became increasingly aware of the impact of the books, which far from being relegates to the scrapbooks of old fashioned children's literature, had become fully woven into American culture. I became convinced from what I read in the archives and other sources, that the Little House books are one of those means by which people in the U.S. learn their political individualism; they are the mother's milk through which Americans ingest their deeply felt individualism. I do not mean to suggest by this that these books are the only source of such ideas; far from it. But I do think that the series, partly because it is not overtly political, does offer powerful although covert instruction. And it does so in a way so as to link the ideas with enormous emotional gratification. Because Wilder and Lane in the stories consistently invest examples of economic and political self-sufficiency with associations of family acceptance and security, I believe that the reader is tempted to conflate the two. Since I have elaborated on this point elsewhere,[3] it is not my main focus here. Instead in this essay I wish to explore the complex means by which these ideas in the books get disseminated in American culture.

Let me begin with just a handful of examples to illustrate my contention that Wilder and Lane carefully reworked their family history so as to emphasize the Ingallses' self-sufficiency and ingenuity and the always destructive role of an intrusive government. For contrast to the stories, I depend upon "Pioneer Girl," Wilder's unpublished nonfiction adult memoir from the late 1920s which is the initial source from which Wilder and Lane drew for the Little House books. I also depend upon the biographical work on Wilder and her family that has been done by such people as William Anderson, William Holtz, John Miller and Ann Romines, and the revisionist history of the American frontiers by scholars like Elizabeth Jameson. Basically what I have argued elsewhere is that although the Little House books are often touted as outstanding frontier history, they are, in actuality, superb examples of the mythology of the American frontier. By that I mean the version of our nation's past that stresses the formative nature of a settlement movement characterized by restlessness, individualism, innovative risk taking, and a propensity to violence, a past largely masculine and Anglo-Saxon in its form, and that has come to take on a symbolizing function that explains us to ourselves.[4]

In regard to the Little House books, I am referring, for instance, to Wilder and Lane's deletion from the stories of the numerous times in which the family lived communally with other people, relatives and nonrelatives, rather than simply on their own, the better to emphasize the family's isolation and independence. The distance from towns of their various homesteads is also exaggerated and the degree to which the girls routinely played with other children is minimized. Because one of the goals of the series is to focus on Ma and Pa's ingenuity in wresting a living from natural resources and from the land, the books downplay the number of times Pa worked for wages. Self-sufficiency and ingenuity, flourishing only when people are left untrammeled by unnecessary regulations, is one of the themes of the series. So whether Ma and Pa are twisting hay for fuel, or grinding seed wheat in a coffee mill, or making apple pie out of green pumpkin, the reader is led to understand that these are unique acts of ingenuity among the Ingalls parents rather than make-do techniques widely shared among frontiers people. Disgusted at the New Deal government interventionist policies to save Americans from situations no worse than those they remembered weathering on their own, Wilder and Lane added scenes to the stories to demonstrate governmental unreliability and destructive meddling. These range from blaming government inconsistency for the Ingalls family's need to leave Kansas, and the reprehensible treatment years later of Uncle Tom and his comrades in the Black Hills, to the chaos at the land office when Pa filed for his homestead claim, to the necessity, because of bureaucratic rules, of a youthful but competent Almanzo to lie about his age to file his claim.

I am aware, of course, that every writer picks and chooses what to put in and what to take out of a story, even if they are working on events that actually happened. No doubt some of the considerations made in regard to the scenes I mentioned were artistic ones, intended to make the stories flow better or be more exciting. And I am also not arguing that political individualism is all that the Little House books are about. Ann Romines has done a splendid job of demonstrating how rich in meaning the books are—as one would expect given the many rereadings they can absorb without boring the reader. Nonetheless, I think the patterns are there, volume after volume, which suggests to me that Wilder and Lane also had ideological purposes in mind as they made their choices, a conviction reinforced by my reading of the correspondence between the two women.

But, even if I can prove beyond the shadow of a doubt that Wilder and Lane put those messages in there, it is much harder to prove that readers take the same messages from the texts that they read. In this essay I will show you some of the building blocks of my efforts to demonstrate that among the melange of ideas and emotions that readers seem to find in the books are those consistent with individualist and anti-government thinking. Keeping in mind my focus on the transmission of ideas, I will look at two areas: first, the use of the books in the elementary school classroom where interpretation of the stories occurs in a largely social setting, and second, the increasingly ubiquitous presence of the books in American culture as interest in the books shifts from a somewhat grassroots phenomenon to a more national and commercial undertaking.

When Terri Lynn Willingham was teaching third grade in the 1980s, she read *Little House in the Big Woods* aloud to her students. Intrigued by this book, Willingham's students clamored for more, so she, a fan herself, read the entire Little House series to them. Because the students were not satisfied even then to let go, she suggested, to their pleasure, a Laura Ingalls Wilder Month. For that month they devoted their entire curriculum to Wilder; all subjects—reading, science, math, social studies, art, music, physical education—emerged from and revolved around the Little House books. Their goal was to put on a week-long program that they would share with the other students in their elementary school.

Their activities ranged from the predictable to the markedly inventive. They became storytellers, retelling Pa's stories to the school's kindergartners. Inspired by the shared adult/student entertainment in the Dakota Territory of Laura's teen years, they organized a school-wide spelling bee in which teachers had to compete, not always successfully, against their own students. Willingham and her class also convinced the physical education teacher to spend the week playing the games mentioned in the books in all his classes and the school dietitian to prepare a typical Ingalls family meal for the whole school. Students wrote their own autobiographies, which went into permanent classroom scrapbooks. They created a life-size reproduction of an 1880s schoolroom with students acting all roles, and designed and made a seven section main exhibit on various aspects of life on the frontier of the 1880s.[5]

Not every teacher or school gives itself over so wholly to Wildermania as did Willingham's—although the thoroughness of her approach is by no means unique—but the Little House books, whether excerpted or full length, are very much a part of today's classroom scene in the United States and have been for many years. Although I cannot demonstrate here the percentage of classrooms in any given year that make some use of the books, my impressionistic evidence suggests that it is at least a significant minority of elementary classes. Of course children individually borrow the books from the library or own their own copies, but collectively they also read, hear, and study them in school, sometimes every year from first or second grade through sixth. Chapters from the books have been included in many of the most popular basal readers for these grades. The books in their entirety are among the preferred texts for a literature-based curriculum, are used as historical sources in social studies units on pioneer life, and form an essential part of even the most rudimentary elementary school library. As in the Willingham classroom, the reading of the books is virtually always connected with some sort of activity, or perhaps even a full range of projects, from quilt and butter making to model log cabin building, and pioneer dress-up. Teachers are offered explicit instructions in the teachers' guides to the basal readers on how to teach the books and they have access to a proliferating number of specific activity guides for the classroom use of the series. Given that we know relatively little about how specific texts are taught to elementary school children, much less interpreted by them, the data for this particular set of books are rich, especially when one adds the several hundred letters that I have read from teachers and children about the use of the books in the classroom.

By the time Terri Willingham introduced Laura Ingalls Wilder to her students, Wilder's stories had already been deemed a valid part of an elementary school education. In fact, one could even say that the books owe their continued presence in American life to teachers and librarians. When the first books in the series were initially published in the early 1930's, librarians and teachers were delighted to have an alternative to the "trashy" but popular Stratemeyer series books such as Nancy Drew and the Hardy Boys.[6] It was largely these professionals who kept the Wilder books alive in the years previous to the spin-off television show and to the current marketing blitz by the books' publisher. Another factor in the books' endurance has to do with the supremacy of the basal reader, introduced at the turn of the century. Basal materials, with carefully chosen reading selections keyed to children's cognitive and social development and accompanied by step-by-step guides for the teacher, were intended to provide "the criteria and materials for scientific reading instruction" whatever the level of teaching instruction or administrative supervision available. Basal reader publishers, according to one scholar, "promised school personnel that all children would learn to read if teachers and students would simply follow the directions supplied in the teacher's guidebook." [7]

Since the 1930's, the dominance of basal readers has been almost complete, despite grassroots resistance on the part of some teachers to their lockstep approach. The trend from the 1960s has been for basal readers to include at least some materials from existing literary works, rather than being composed entirely of stories written especially for the readers. The Little House books have profited from their long-favored status with librarians, teachers, critics, and children, for selections from the books have been excerpted in dozens of basal readers, many of them by major publishers, for both primary and middle grades. Oral discussion, vocabulary lists, grammar explanations, workbook assignments, and book reports are all activities teachers are advised in the teacher's guides to append to the reading of the Little House chapter or chapters offered in the texts. One scholar maintains that from the 1960s to 1990, "over 90 percent of elementary school teachers use[d] basals over 90 percent of the time during reading instruction."[8]

While the Little House books are part of the curriculum in the sense that they are included in many basal readers, there is no school district that I am aware of that mandates that all children should have studied the books before they graduate. If the books are utilized extensively in many classrooms across the country, it is not only that because they have been given the seal of professional approval, but also because teachers themselves are fiercely committed to the series, often based on their own childhood experiences with it. When it comes time in the community of the classroom to ascribe meaning to these books, the teacher's role is very important. Research has indicated that an instructor's clearly expressed appreciation of a book lends "a special sanction to its use." There is ample evidence to suggest that the choices of books that teachers make for their classrooms, the access to those books and the presentation and discussion of them affect the responses expressed by the children, both in quantity and quality.[9] Thus a teacher's clear passion for the Little House series, her willingness to read and display the books, to have copies available for her students, and to undertake interesting class projects based on the books, all signal to the students that it will be worth their while to open themselves to the books and to develop their thoughts about them.

If we were to go into a primary or middle school, we might find teachers using the Wilder books in a variety of ways, both formal and informal. In the latter category are those teachers who read one or more of the books aloud to their students following a return from recess or during other ritualized "calm-down" periods. Some children read along in their own copies of the books while others just listen attentively. The feelings of well-being and relaxation that this activity induces in children seems to create very positive associations with the Little House books, associations which some teachers go out of their way to cultivate. One teacher at a private school has had a fireplace with electric logs built for her classroom. As students enter the classroom in the morning and when the teacher "read[s] Laura" after lunch, candles and kerosene lamps on the mantle provide the only light in the room. Her students love the coziness of this corner.[10] But even without such dramatic changes to their classrooms, students writing to their former teachers many years later sometimes refer to those Little House reading rituals as the most memorable part of elementary school life.[11] I would argue that this context affects children's responses to the books.

For decades many teachers have been reading aloud to their classes, but only in recent years have reading experts come to believe that "reading aloud is the single most influential factor in young children's success in learning to read."[12] Increasingly the professional literature for teachers has also stressed the importance of "book talk" in providing "children with space to explore their initial responses to literature," in learning "new strategies for evoking and responding to literature," and in participating "in constructing shared, enriched interpretations of literature."[13] Although apparently it is a struggle to get teachers to move beyond a fact-testing question and answer approach in which they dominate, some teachers have become very careful about encouraging less structured discussion following the reading aloud session, whether by the entire class, in small groups, or in reading journals.   From their letters to me, I surmise that many teachers are drawn to the association of contentment with the lack of material goods conveyed by the books. "I read the books mainly to stress the idea that 'things don't make people content,'" a fifth grade Florida teacher wrote me.[14] Other teachers emphasize the resilience of the Ingalls family unit, its ability to survive under stress, a theme that some of them feel resonates with their own students.[15] Do teachers introduce their interpretations of the stories into these book talks? I can't answer this question with any certainty, but I have a hard time believing that all teachers refrain from such a temptation. That doesn't mean, however, that children don't also influence each other in these discussions; from recorded conversations about other books, we can see that they do.

Reading aloud, book talk. All that is in contrast to the more formalized approach to the books imposed by the basal readers and various teachers' guides, sources upon which teachers depend heavily.[16] In those classrooms—surely the majority of those using some part of the Wilder books—reading is more likely to be done largely by the children on their own and is less likely to be followed by discussion, than by completing fact based exercises in their workbooks. Certainly reading children's answers to such questions yields little clue as to what meaning they have given to the stories. In the interests of sales, textbook publishers seek to underplay any ideological or even faintly controversial aspect to their books. Usually the textbook compilers include chapters from the Wilder books that are engaging on their own, requiring no knowledge of the entire book or series to make them appealing. That means that episodes that are funny, exciting, or suspenseful are the most likely choices. And indeed, gauging from their letters to me written from the classroom, students do seem to respond positively to these aspects of the stories, liking depictions of dangers overcome.

Nonetheless, there are certain patterns that one can see in the selection of Little House excerpts that appear in the basal readers. Virtually every chapter from the series included in the readers can be interpreted as contributing in some way to the overall picture of individual and family initiative and self-sufficiency and Laura and her sisters' sense of security and family good feeling. A commonly excerpted chapter is from *On the Banks of Plum Creek* in which Laura immerses herself in a bubbling, rain swollen creek and almost drowns. The experience makes her realize that although the creek is beyond human control and that there are things stronger than anybody, the creek did not vanquish her: "It had not made her scream and it could not make her cry."[17] A grade five reader includes the chapters from *By the Shores of Silver Lake* in which the family, for money, houses and feeds hundreds of men coming into Dakota Territory to stake claims, and in which Pa goes off to file his own claim. These chapters might be said to show the Ingallses' enterprise and initiative, their habit of just going ahead and making the best of less than ideal conditions, and in the story of Pa's experiences at the land office, show also the chaos and violence attendant upon any government sponsored activity.[18] Another fifth grade reader includes the chapter from *The Long Winter* describing how Laura and Carrie are almost lost on the prairie during a blizzard because they must stay with their classmates who are following two incompetent adults trying to lead them from the schoolhouse back into town. The implications of this selection might be that following the group is a mistake and that no matter how impossible it seems to go on in difficult conditions, it is necessary, and in the end, possible to do so. That close call is immediately followed by an extended description of the girls' comfort and well-being in the midst of their family when they finally get home—the pattern that I believe characterizes all the books.[19]

While I doubt that many children or teachers consciously perceive a politically individualist message in the stories, they do pick up the message about the importance of initiative and persistence. Research is divided on whether U.S. children's books as a whole are biased toward individualist or cooperative resolution of crises, but the belief among researchers is that teachers themselves seem to favor texts with individualistic solutions.[20] Both basal readers and teachers inform children that the Little House books are true, i.e., that the Laura in the stories is Laura Ingalls Wilder and that the stories are based on her real experiences as a child. If there is one consistent motif that runs through children's oral and written responses to the books, it is this one, the realness of the stories, the wonder of being able to know in such minute detail about people in the past. This translates into children's sense that they are learning the true history of pioneers, a belief that is reinforced by the frequent use of the books in social studies units and in situations like Terri Willingham's classroom, use across all the disciplines from music to science. Thus, if the Ingallses confronted challenges and dangers on their own, so was it the case, presumably, for pioneers in general.

In virtually all cases, the reading of the books is accompanied by other, hands-on activities, which I would argue contributes to students' sense of the truth of the books. In the professional literature they read, teachers are told over and over of the importance of activity in learning. As one influential text on children's literature puts it, "We know that it is important for children learning basic math concepts to manipulate concrete materials. In a similar way, children extend their understanding of literature when they have an opportunity to represent and manipulate the elements of literature in some concrete form," whether it be drawings, drama, story making, etc. The authors of this text remind their readers of the Chinese proverb: "I hear and I forget/I see and I remember/I do and I understand."[21]

     Writing specifically of the Little House books, another teacher commented that when she realized that her students didn't understand fully everything mentioned in the books, she concluded that they "would benefit from a tangible approach" to the books. In her case, as in many others, this meant selecting activities described in the stories for replication in the classroom.[22] Even if they don't go to the extremes of Willingham's class, I doubt that there is a class in the U.S. that has read the stories without making butter from whipping cream, building models of log cabins or covered wagons, or making quilts in some form. Many others have ground seed wheat in coffee grinders, made and worn sunbonnets, sung songs mentioned in the books, and devised plays based on the stories. If the literature is correct, then these activities do affect student comprehension of the stories and make more complex their responses to them. Certainly these activities reinforce the sense of the truth of the books, for if the stories can be relied upon for instructions as to how to make butter or a button lamp—and these how-to parts of the books are especially beloved by children—then the less tangible information in the books must also be true. The lessons that children seem to draw from the books' many descriptions of material deprivation, in combination with their own novice attempts to make a few foods from scratch and goods by hand, is that the crucial difference between today and the past is that people of the past led hard and deprived lives, although they also seemed to have fun and to have close families. "If the pioneers saw us, they would think we are spoiled brats," one sixth grader from New Jersey commented, perhaps summing up the older students' ambivalent responses to the past, their sense of guilty pleasure in having life easier.[23] Despite their teachers' earnest attempts to equate happiness with few material possessions, for every child who wishes to be Laura Ingalls Wilder, or Laura's friend, there are many others who declare themselves relieved not to live in such hard times, lacking TV and MacDonalds.

I have gone into some detail here on the use of the books in the classroom, partly because school is the place where many Americans are introduced to the Little House books and because in general people do not realize how integral these books are to the curriculum in many classrooms. Children hone their language arts skills on the books, as well as learn from them about the "real" pioneer experience. I have also dwelt on the classroom because from this one controlled example of how a community of readers creates meaning from a text, we can see how complex a process this is and how important context is to what individuals take from a text. Certainly their familiarity with the books and their likely positive associations with them may predispose children to respond with interest to references to Wilder and to the series that they encounter outside the classroom.

And encounter them they do. This brings me to my second focal point, an examination of the dissemination of the Wilder books in the general American culture. The books have become common cultural currency, signaling in a host of ways the beleaguered core of presumable traditional American values. The series has taken on a life of its own that sometimes does not depend upon reading the stories. The most obvious (although not the only) example of this is the television program, "Little House on the Prairie." That program was different enough from the books to make any generalizations about shared or dissimilar ideas in the two formats the worthy topic of a separate study. Suffice it to say here that the television program has served to introduce many Americans—not to mention others around the world—to the series and to Wilder as an iconic figure. Certainly it succeeded in raising the profile of the Little House books from the 1970's on.

That doesn't mean that the Little House books were not a fundamental part of many readers' lives from the publication of the first volumes. In the days before kids' paperback books and the casual acquisition of books for children, it was a cherished Christmas ritual for Wilder's young fans to receive one of the hardbound volumes in the series each December. Early in the life of the series, children began acting out the stories, sometimes squabbling over whom should be Laura and who Mary. In the case of one girl in Minneapolis in 1946, appropriately, this activity took place in a log cabin playhouse her father built out of trees that he himself cut down. As early as the 1950s, a play based on the books was presented occasionally in De Smet, South Dakota although the pageant itself did not begin until 1971. In 1948 a pair of child fans from Minneapolis had already done an Ingalls tour, visiting De Smet, Keystone, and

Pierre.[24] By and large, however, in the years before the television program the books largely came into people's lives and into popular culture through programs in libraries and classrooms, through the still nascent efforts of the various Laura Ingalls Wilder memorial societies and commemorative stamp campaigns, and through the private activities of individuals—or in the case of William Anderson, public activities. Since the mid-1970's there has been an explosion of Wilder and Little House material into many aspects of American life. I won't have the opportunity to explore them all in this essay, but I think I will be able to make my point that the books are woven into the fabric of American life in ways that deepen their importance to their fans and make them synonymous with the pioneer experience even to the person who has only indirect familiarity with them.

We are all so used to fads that are strictly the creation of marketing departments of giant corporations, that it is important to recall that until the recent marketing campaign on the part of HarperCollins, the passion for the Little House books felt by readers had been almost entirely a grassroots phenomenon, generated by readers themselves, a fact that may well have affected the meaning attached to the stories. Many of the Little House-related products and events have been the outcome of supply emerging to meet real, not manufactured demand. Yes, the books have long been available in inexpensive book club editions through schools, but that by itself doesn't explain the steadily growing number of individuals and families who have been visiting the Ingalls and Wilder homesites since the 1940s, numbering several thousand in the early 1970's, growing to 12,000 –15,000 (depending on the site) after the first seasons of the television program, and now, long after the show has passed into rerun land, swelling to 40,000 visitors annually at the more popular sites.[25] Devotees have come in nineteenth century dress, in convoys of recreational vehicles, in family groupings of four generations. It is because the books have become so important to readers that they have been eager to see the places where Wilder actually lived and to learn more details about her life both during and after the time covered by the books.

Children as well as adults have persistently integrated the stories into their lives. A mother reported in the 1990's that her young daughters made their assigned household tasks tolerable by pretending to be Laura and Mary who did such tasks without complaining.[26] Many people seem to find it impossible to endure a severe winter storm without comparing themselves to the Ingalls family. One seven year-old boy, driving with his mother in rush hour during a snowstorm, wondered aloud what Pa Ingalls would make of their situation.[27] In 1994, a woman in Rosedale, Mississippi who had been without electricity for two weeks because of an ice storm, was given "A Little House on the Prairie" medal by her friends.[28] A woman from Marshalltown, Iowa found the stories to have practical application: Based on what she recalled from *The Long Winter*, she tied a rope between her back door and her garage to avoid getting lost during a 1996 blizzard. She also learned another lesson from the books: Because the county's services during the storm were so unsatisfactory, she and her neighbors vowed to secede from the county and pay their taxes directly to the enterprising neighbor who had used his snow plow to clear their roads and driveways when the county was lax.[29] Rose Wilder Lane—and possibly her mother as well—would have cheered. A Ph.D. student in anthropology from Rochester, New York spent two years living in a tiny, remote Russian village, partially making sense of the experience by comparing it to the pioneer adventures recounted by Wilder.[30] Other readers, seeing her as a match or inspiration for their own spunkiness or as a general role model, have turned Laura into themselves, their best friends, their mothers. "I feel I was raised by three people—Mom, Dad, and Laura Ingalls Wilder!" one young woman mused.[31]

Adults as well as children have used the books for comfort, reading them again and again, sometimes as substitution for the warm family life they themselves lack and sometimes as solace in hard times. A newspaper columnist recalled the positive childhood associations she had with the annual Christmas gift from her mother of one of the Little House books. Her description of plunging into the new book right in the midst of the holiday chaos at her house is salted with words like "cozy," "comfort," "snug." "I must admit," one less fortunate woman wrote to me of her childhood, "that my family life was not as happy as in the books; however when things got tough, I could always steal away to my room and escape to another few chapters in a Little House book."[32] Another woman, struggling through the long winters of Massachusetts indicates that she reads the whole set every winter, that the books are like an anti-depressant for her, while a sixty-eight-year-old man writes that he rereads the books as a "word tranquilizer" for the "renewal of [his] spirit."[33] Other readers have used the books to get themselves through potentially depressing periods of illness, injury or other disasters. In 1950, ten-year-old Californian Kim Chernin added a Little House book to the change of clothing and the candy bar in the small emergency bag she maintained in case her communist parents were deported or arrested and she had to run away.[34] As you might imagine, given my thesis of the books' conflation of political individualism with family good feeling, I consider these associations of the books with comfort to be significant. The books make people—or more specifically white people—feel good.[35] As one forty-seven-year old white male fan informed me in a single breath, the books give him "piecefullness [sic] and tranquility" [sic] even as they demonstrate that in Laura's childhood, "They didn't have welfair [sic] and food stamps as we have now [so] each family had to pull together and take care of each other."[36]

But the books don't just make people feel good; they push them into action. As Barbara M. Walker puts it, "Laura Ingalls Wilder's way of describing her pioneer childhood seemed to compel participation." Walker and her daughter began making every food mentioned in the books, and Walker notes, "From other mothers I learned that our impulses were far from unique." She did push her impulses further than most, however; she wrote the splendid *The Little House Cookbook*.[37] Other fans' forms of participation have been less public. An eleven-year-old girl opened the Laura Ingalls Wilder Shelf and Museum. Located in her bedroom, she had welcomed twenty-five visitors when she wrote me in late 1993.[38] A thirty-seven-year-old woman in Washington state changed her name legally from Nancy to Carrie in honor of the books and had sought out a farm where she could help take care of cows like Laura did.[39] Other readers inspired by the books have taken up the violin, have developed an interest in history and/or antiques, undertaken 4-H projects based on incidents in the books, entered history fair competitions focused on Wilder, written books inspired by the series (in fact, it has been estimated that by 1979, there were 100 children's prairie homesteading stories, all based on the Little House prototype). Inspired readers have also built, by hand, elaborate log cabins in which to live, and have cut down on the number and elaborateness of their Christmas presents. There is a sizable sorority and small fraternity of individuals who, as either amateurs or professionals, make presentations in libraries and schools all over the country on Wilder and the books. There seems also to be a strong correlation between the homeschooling movement and enthusiasm for the Little House books. It is notable that the best and most thorough child level study guide to the books are the two volumes written by Ann Dahl for the Calvert School which produces much curriculum for homeschoolers.[40] A homeschooling mother in Louisiana engaged not only her daughter's attention in the books, but also her husband's: "It seems amazing that Laura's life can touch us so that we just must be a part of it in some small way."[41]

Probably the most significant transition from fan to active proponent of the books is to be found in William Anderson's life. One could do a whole essay on his role in making the Little House books and the Ingalls,

Wilder, and Lane families part of American culture. I suspect that at times he must wonder what he got himself into all those years ago. Here I want to mention just one activity with which he has been associated over the years: the commemorative stamp campaign. The first signs of such a campaign emerged in 1966; its petitioners naively hoped that they could get a Laura Ingalls Wilder stamp issued in time for the centenary of her birth in 1967. In conjunction with the Wilder home in Mansfield, Missouri, Anderson tried again in 1970; schoolchildren, zealous fans, and a children's booksellers association were all part of subsequent campaigns which resulted in a partial victory in 1993: the issuing of a stamp series celebrating four beloved classics of American children's literature, including *Little House on the Prairie*.[42]

While not every example of Wilder's or the books' place in American culture is an outgrowth of the action of fans, many are. The numerous library branches and elementary and middle schools named after her or one of the books are often efforts to be responsive to popular feeling. The steady stream of Wilder fans passing through small towns in the Upper Midwest on their way to the various homesites has pushed county governments to try to partake of some of the tourist bounty. The highways connecting the sites in Wisconsin, Minnesota, South Dakota and Iowa have recently been designated the Laura Ingalls Wilder Historic Highway.[43]

Gradually, activities which had been amateur and individual, are becoming professionalized—and more visible. This is both the inevitable outcome of the years of pent-up interest in the books and the belated realization on the part of commercial interests that there is big money to be made. There are still as many former teachers and librarians and long-time fans as there ever were doing library and classroom one-woman shows, but now there are also numerous professional or semi-professional theatrical productions—many of them musicals—based on various aspects of Wilder's life, or dramatized versions of incidents in the books.[44] Chautauquas, those mind-elevating cultural events for the hinterlands dating back to the last quarter of the nineteenth century, have recently been revived, this time using professional actors to capture the personalities and ideas of historic figures. This has put "Laura Ingalls Wilder" in company on the lecture circuit with the likes of such cultural icons as Henry David Thoreau, Emily Dickinson, Buffalo Bill Cody, Willa Cather, F. Scott Fitzgerald, and Mark Twain.[45] Once children's drawings of characters and scenes from the Little House books might have lined the walls of elementary schools. Now, however, in Grand Prairie School in Frankfort, Illi-

nois, the first of twenty-five planned murals by professional artists and
their school children assistants has been completed and welcomes you at
the main entrance. What is this first mural? The Ingalls family in their
covered wagon crossing the prairie.[46] There are still tens of thousands of
families retracing, on their own, the Ingalls and Wilder families' migrations every summer. Since the late 1970s, various educational institutions
have offered credit courses during the summer based on following the
Ingallses' 1600 mile trail of sites from Pepin and Mansfield to DeSmet.
Often the students have been teachers and librarians who then have brought
back fresh ideas to the classrooms. The mid 1990s brought a commer-
cially organized one-week "Pioneering Women" tour, following in the footsteps of Willa Cather, Mari Sandoz, and Laura Ingalls Wilder. The Wilder
connection has been the tour's main lure from the beginning.[47] And how
could I not mention The Little House collector dolls (with their brown-eyed
Laura) as replacements for, or are they supplements to, those low-tech
versions of Charlotte that many girls cherished? Computer technology
has given us new means to indulge our interest in the books. E-mail discussion lists devoted to Wilder and the books provide opportunities for
information exchange, discussion, and disagreement. There are dozens or
web sites, devoted to Wilder, including one put together by a young woman
who started off as a child playing Laura and Mary with a friend.[48]

   Clearly then, there are many elements at play here. Through all
these means: children's study of the books in school, the transformative
effects of child and adult passion for the books, the gradual emergence of
the books from the status of underground classics promoted by small scale
and informal means to a ubiquitous presence on the American landscape,
now tied in to numerous commercial enterprises, the Little House books
have become synonymous with the American frontier past—at times even
with all things rural. They are firmly linked to family values, with the
haziness that phrase entails, to deprivation bravely endured and to an appreciation of simple pleasures. As a California woman doing the "Laura
tour" with her son in 1998 put it, "I like the simplicity of the life, the
traditional values and the family unity."[49] Time after time newspaper and
magazine writers start with an anecdote or generalization drawn from the
Little House books or a reference to Wilder as a teaser to draw readers
into their story, apparently certain that the reference will be self-evident.
An article about inexpensive holiday meals in New York City begins with
a quote from Wilder about being happy with simple pleasures. A piece on
baby boomers' willingness to pursue unfulfilled dreams even in middle age
is begun by a reference to Laura Ingalls Wilder starting her novel writing

in her sixties. In a feature on Women's History Month, a writer for the *Chicago Sun-Times* leads off with Wilder as one of the many Midwestern women who have made a mark on history.[50]

And then there are the articles and events in which the Little House books are not merely the lead-in but serve as a means by which Americans interpret past and present. While there are occasional warnings that the books are not appropriate guides for us today, the overwhelming majority of sources, drawing on very partial readings of the series, suggest the opposite, that we would be well-advised to look to the Ingallses' and Wilders' lives for guidance. Two recent op-ed columns in the pages of major newspapers either bemoaned the diminished importance of fathers in their children's lives in comparison to the central role that Pa Ingalls played, or berated us and our schools for not teaching our children as effectively, in both content and motivation, as Laura was taught.[51] The message is clear that something in the combination of cohesive families with uniform goals and the absence of insidious indulgences led to better functioning citizens in the past. Another constant refrain expresses the anxiety that it is our modern conveniences that have lured us into lives destructive to family, peace of mind, and to the environment. Folks back in the late nineteenth century, without all our modern conveniences, "found time for hearth and home, family and church, work and play." As another commentator put it, "can we even imagine what those brave souls [i.e. the pioneers] would have thought of today's family life?"[52]

Almost seventy years after the first book in the series was published, the Little House books, far from being artifacts of juvenile literary history, are a deeply entrenched part of U.S. culture. From childhood to old age, Americans encounter the books and their author in a wide variety of contexts. Whether they are fans or simply members of the public, they will find it hard to escape the books or reference to them altogether. Individual fans may draw a variety of implications from the stories, but the range of meanings assigned publicly to the books has been decidedly narrow and heavily sentimentalized. There is much more to the stories than has been suggested in most forums. We will never understand the books' impact nor their importance until we look at the books, their author(s), and their presence in American history and life more carefully, with a kind of loving dispassionateness.

As I hope I have demonstrated, the place of Little House books in American culture is constantly evolving. That is why I have high hopes for a symposium like this one. I would like to see the more complex views of Wilder, the Little House books, and the American frontier as portrayed by John Miller, Ann Romines, Elizabeth Jameson, William Anderson, and yes, myself, become part of the bank of meanings upon which we all draw when we dwell upon, and in, the Little House books.

Endnotes

1. J. Richard Piper, *Ideologies and Institutions: American Conservative and Liberal Governance Prescriptions Since 1933* (Lanham, MD: Rowman & Littlefield Publishers Inc., 1997), 110-119; Godfrey Hodgson, *The World Turned Right Side Up: A History of the Conservative Ascendancy in America* (Boston: Houghton Mifflin, 1996), 17-18, 85-87; Barry D. Karl, *The Uneasy State* (Chicago: University of Chicago Press, 1983), 226; Nathan Glazer, "Individualism and Equality In the United States," *Making America: The Society and Culture of the United States*, ed. Luther S. Luedtke (Chapel Hill: University of North Carolina Press, 1992): 300. This is not to deny the persistence of an antipathy to government planning and a skepticism about most regulatory and social welfare policies on the part of many conservatives in these years. Piper points out that "libertarian and traditionalist brands of conservatism waged an internal battle for the soul of the conservative movement, a battle that has never ended despite varied efforts at fusion." Piper, *Ideologies and Institutions*, 392.

2. Karl writes of "our commitment to the autonomous individual as the fundamental element in American democracy." *The Uneasy State*, 7.

3. Anita Clair Fellman, "Laura Ingalls Wilder and Rose Wilder Lane: The Politics of a Mother-Daughter Relationship," *Signs: Journal of Women in Culture and Society* 15, no. 3 (1990): 535-561.

4. Fellman, "'Don't Expect to Depend on anybody Else': The Frontier as Portrayed in the Little House Books," *Children's Literature* 24, ed. Francelia Butler, R.H.W. Dillard, and Elizabeth Lenox Keyser (New Haven: Yale University Press, 1996), 101-116.

5. Terri Lynn Willingham, "Frontiers for Learning," *Learning: Creative Ideas and Insights for Teachers* 16, no. 6 (1988): 49-51.

6. Nancy Tillman Romalov, "Children's Series Books and the Rhetoric of Guidance: A Historical Overview," *Rediscovering Nancy Drew*, Carolyn Stewart Dyer and Nancy Tillman Romalov, eds. (Iowa City: University of Iowa Press, 1995), 118.

7. Patrick Shannon, "Basal Readers and Illusion of Legitimacy," in *Textbooks in American Society*, ed. Philip G. Altbach, et al. (Albany: State University of New York Press, 1991), 222.

8. Ibid. 223. Also see Charlotte Huck, "Literature-Based Reading Programs: A Retrospective," *The New Advocate* 9, no. 1 (1996): 23-33.

9. Janet Hickman, "Everything Considered: Response to Literature in an Elementary School Setting," *Journal of Research and Development in Education* 16, no. 3 (1983): 12.

10. Ann Dahl, letter to William T. Anderson, 22 December 1997.

11. Ethel Stutzman, letter to author, 9 October 1992

12. R. Routman, *Invitations: Changing as Teachers and Learners K-12* (Portsmouth, NH: Heinemann, 1991), quoted in Veronica Gonzalex, et al., "Our Journey Toward Better Conversations About Books," in Nancy L. Roser and Miriam G. Martinez, eds, *Book Talk and Beyond: Children and Teachers Respond to Literature* (Newark, DE: International Reading Association, 1995), 170.

13. Lea M. McGee, "Talking About Books with Young Children," in Roser and Martinez, eds, *Book Talk and Beyond*, 114.

14. Boyd Peart, letter to author, 5 October 1992; also Marily Dewald, letter to author, 15 January 1993.

15. Patricia Conway, letter to author, n.d. (ca. 1992-93).

16. Jere E. Brophy, "How Teachers Influence What is Taught and Learned in Classrooms," *The Elementary School Journal* 83, no. 1 (Summer 1982): 12.

17. "The Footbridge," [from *On the Banks of Plum Creek*] in *Dreams and Dragons*, Teacher's Edition (New York: Harper & Row Publishers, 1976), 269-278.

18. "By the Shores of Silver Lake" in *Landscapes*, Teacher's Edition (New York: Macmillan, 1987), 174-187.

19. "Blizzard!" [from *The Long Winter*] in *Moccasins and Marvels*, Teacher's Edition (New York: Harper & Row, 1976), 260-267.

20. Patrick Shannon, "Hidden Within the Pages: A Study of Social Perspective in Young Children's Favorite Books," *The Reading Teacher* 39, no. 7 (March 1986): 656-63; Kathleen A. J. Mohr, "Metamessages and Problem-Solving Perspectives in Children's Literature," *Reading Horizons* 33, no. 4 (1993): 342-46.

21. Charlotte S. Huck, Susan Hepler, and Janet Hickman, *Children's Literature in the Elementary School*, 4th ed. (N.Y.: Holt, Rinehart & Winston, 1987), 678.

22. Barbara Steinberger, "Learning about 'Little House'" *Childhood Education* 57 (Jan.-Feb. 1981): 161-64.

23. Sixth grade girl; letter to author, 23 March 1993.

24. *Dear Laura: Letters from Children to Laura Ingalls Wilder* (New York: HarperCollins Publishers, Inc., 1996), 72, 141, 82.

25. *Laura Ingalls Wilder Lore* 2. No. 2 (1976): 1. Over 600 people attended the June 1979 dedication of the Little House Wayside at Laura's birthplace in Pepin, Wisconsin. *Laura Ingalls Wilder Lore* 5, no. 2 (1979): 4.

26. Shelby Anne Wolf and Shirley Brice Heath, "The Net of Story," *The Horn Book Magazine* 69, no. 6 (Nov./Dec. 1993): 707.

27. Barbara Edwards, "'Wouldn't Pa Be Amazed!' Connecting with Literature Through Conversation," *The New Advocate* 4, no. 4 (Fall 1991): 247; also see Corene Phillips's account in "Nebraska's 'Blizzard of '96'" in *Kearney Hue*, January 23, 1996.

28. National Public Radio, *Morning Edition*, 25 February 1994.

29. Rose Kodet, "Is That Whining in the Background a Snow Blower?" *Marshalltown* [Iowa] *Times-Republican*, 16 February 1996.

30. "Russian Resolution," *Rochester* [NY] *Democrat and Chronicle*, 18 February 1996.

31. Kathleen O'Connell, letter to author, 11 February 1994; also see Gabrielle Anne Wiegand, letter to William T. Anderson, n.d., indicating "I wish I knew Laura. I wish I was Laura." Also see Robyn Hallett, letter to William T. Anderson, 10 November 1993.

32. Maggie Lewis, "Snuggle Up to a Pioneer Story," *The Christian Science Monitor*, 24 August 1993, The Home Forum Section; Laura Waskin, letter to author, 28 November 1993.

33. Marsha Gustafson, letter to author, 4 March 1994; Otis Disworth, letter to author, 16 December 1993; also see Diane Lanclot, letter to author, 13 January 1994.

34. Kim Chernin, *In My Mother's House: A Daughter's Story* (New York: Harper & Row Publishers, 1983), 217.

35. I will not be able to deal with the issue in this essay, but I suggest that the relationship of readers of color to the books is much more problematic.

36. John Pascarella, letter to author, 1993.

37. Barbara M. Walker, *The Little House Cookbook: Frontier Foods from Laura Ingalls Wilder's Classic Stories* (New York: Harper & Row, 1979), xiv.

38. Diana Rissetto, letter to author, 15 December 1993.

39. Carrie Aadland, letter to author, 19 November 1993.

40. *The Little House Books Reading Guide*, Vols. 1&2 (Calvert School, 1994).

41. Sandra Petit, letter to William T. Anderson, 15 May 1992; also see Kelley O'Conor, letter to author, 19 October 1992; Randi Rice, "Schooling at Home: More Parents Opting to Teach Their Children," *The Atlanta Journal and Constitution*, 2 January 1991, sec. J, 7; Jessica Schild, "Homeschoolers Hold Cultural Fair," *Norway* [Maine] *Advertiser Democrat*, 25 January 1996.

42. *Laura Ingalls Wilder Lore* 7, no. 1 (1981): 2; *Laura Ingalls Wilder Lore*, 6, no. 2 (1980): 3; Judith Vogt, letter to William Anderson, 18 November 1986; David Kristy, letter to William Anderson, 22 May 1989.

43. Judith Vogt, letter to William Anderson, 18 November 1986, David Kristy, letter to William Anderson, 22 May 1989.

44. Valerie Takahama, "Young, Old See Wilder's 'Little House,'" *The Orange County Register*, 23 November 1992, sec. B, 3; "On the Towns, "*New York Times*, 14 January 1996, New Jersey edition sec. 13, 12; "Arts Schedule," *St. Louis Post-Dispatch*, 29 August 1996, Get Out Section, 28; "On the Towns," *New York Times*, 29, September 1996, New Jersey edition, sec 13, 13; Damien Jaques, "La Dolce DeVita," *Milwaukee Journal Sentinel,* 23 November 1995, Cue Section, 1; Todd Kreidler, "Theaters Remember Christmas is for Kids," *Pittsburgh Post-Gazette*, 12 December 1996, sec. B, 2; Terry Doran, "Noteworthy, *The Buffalo News*, 14 November 1997, sec. G, 14; Doran, "Wilder Things: Building the Christmas Spirit on the Prairie," *The Buffalo News*, 21 November 1997, sec. G 25; Jim Delmont, "'Little House' Emphasizes Warm, Fuzzy," *Omaha World-Herald*, 29 November 1997, Living Today Section, 71; Robert Trussell, "'Little House' Gives the Gift of Christmas Past," *The Kansas City Star*, 28 November 1997, Preview Section, 19; Helen Holzer, "Laura Comes to Life," *The Atlanta Journal and Constitution*, 21 February 1998, sec. LG, 16; Paula Voell, "Laura Lives," *The Buffalo News*, 23

April 1998, sec. B, 1.

45. Doug Pokorski, "Heartland Chautauqua Returns to New Salem," *Springfield* [Illinois] *The State Journal-Register*, 1 June 1998, Local section, 16; Aaron Deck, "One for the Books," *The Phoenix Arizona Republic*, 1 April 1998, 12.

46. Mary Ellen Michna, "What They See is What They Read," *Chicago Tribune*, April 20, 1997, Southwest edition, Tempo sec., 3.

47. Mary Ellen Graff, "A 'Wilder Weekend'" *Laura Ingalls Wilder Lore*, 3, no. 2 (1977): 3; Also see her follow-up article in 10, no. 1 (1984): 5. Information on other study tours appears in *Laura Ingalls Wilder Lore* 5, no.2 (1999): 4, and 11, no. 1 (1985): 3. On the commercial tour see Marla Paul, "Novel Tour Lets You Trek the Trails of Pioneers," *Chicago Tribune*, 23 July 1995, Womanews sec., 6; "Her Story," *Pittsburgh Post-Gazette*, 6 April 1997, sec. F, 2.

48. Rebecca Irby and Rachel Hatcher, letter to William T. Anderson, n.d.

49. Beth Gauper, "Fans Seek Out Little Sites on the Prairie," *The Des Moines Register*, 3 May 1998, Travel sec., 3.

50. Sylvia Carter, "Dining Down to Earth" *Newsday*, 23 December 1992, Food sec., 61; Don O'Briant, "Baby Boom Generation is Discovering that You're Never Too Old," *The Orange County Register*, 4 November 1992, sec. E, 3; Mi-Ai Ahern, "Digging into Midwest Women's Contributions," *Chicago Sun-Times*, Sunday, 1 March 1998, Travel sec., 1.

51. Rick Shefchik, "Dad's Homecoming on the Prairie was a Major Family Event," *St. Louis Post-Dispatch*, 15 June 1997, sec. B, 3; Barbara P. Jones, "Instruct Students Well and Demand Master," *The Washington Post*, 26 September 1996, sec, A, 31. Also see Julie Anderson, "Making School Work Count," *St. Louis Parent*, February 1996.

52. Victoria Hecht, "Just Keep it Simple in 1996," *Virginia Beach Sun*, 5 January 1996; Jeanne Larson, "Fiddlin' Around Finlayson," *Pine County* [Minnesota] *Courier*, 18 January 1996. Also see Hannah Holmes, "Gifts from the Earth," *The Montreal Gazette*, 21 December 1991, sec. I, 8.

Unconscious Inheritance and Conscious Striving: Laura Ingalls Wilder and the Frontier Narrative

ELIZABETH JAMESON

> Each nation has bequeathed something to its successors; no age has suffered the highest content of the past to be lost entirely. By unconscious inheritance and by conscious striving after the past as part of the present, history has acquired continuity.
> Frederick Jackson Turner, 1891
> "The Significance of History"

In 1893, a young historian born on the Wisconsin frontier announced his revisionist interpretation of American history. America, Frederick Jackson Turner insisted, did not simply grow from European "germs," or seeds. Rather, he asserted, American history was "in a large degree the history of the colonization of the Great West. The existence of an area of free land, its continuous recession, and the advance of American settlement westward," he said, "explain American development."[1]

Some fifty years later, in 1941, George Wilson Pierson of Yale University surveyed professional historians' assessments of Frederick Jackson Turner's frontier thesis. Among 106 replies was one, Pierson reported, from "[o]ne of the deans of our profession," who pointed out "that Turner's theory is overwhelmingly a masculine one, with the role of women in Western settlement almost entirely neglected." "Whether or not the hypothesis will have to be modified, when the feminine role is studied," Pierson commented, "is a question that American historians may some day have to face."[2]

"Some day" took awhile. Eighteen years passed before another historian addressed the significance of an all-male frontier, when David Potter asked whether its celebrated individualism and freedom applied to women.[3] By identifying as "masculine" those qualities that Turner called "American," Potter opened a history of frontier and gender. Serious examinations of pioneer women date from the late 1970s. We are still sifting what frontiers meant for many women, who were generally outnumbered by men and often isolated from other women. Women pioneers often characterized the frontier period as far-from-liberating, a time consumed with the dual burdens of settlement and childbearing. Their own accounts located freedom after the frontier, when work was lighter and civilized institutions more accessible.[4]

If it took almost a century for historians to add the "feminine role" to western history, our most enduring image of that "feminine role" was virtually intact when Pierson conducted his survey. In 1941, *Little Town on the Prairie* was published, the seventh volume in Laura Ingalls Wilder's eight-volume children's novel that introduced many Americans to the intimate world of a young girl's family-centered frontier. As one reviewer noted when *The First Four Years* appeared in 1971, Wilder has "given a notion of what pioneer life was like to far more Americans than ever heard of Frederick Jackson Turner."[5]

Certainly millions more have read Wilder.[6] But Turner's frontier shaped an enduring narrative of national history. Wilder added "the feminine role" and the intimate world of a loving family to create an inviting and enticing image of pioneer life. The combined promise of frontier opportunity and a secure family shaped many children's images of pioneer America. I inherited that story with my own set of Little House books, which my grandmother gave me, a book at a time, after Harpers published a new edition in 1953. The Little House books constructed a version of frontier America with which I could identify, in which I vicariously participated, and which probably influenced my professional preoccupation with western women's histories. And so in 1993, when I was asked to speak on women and the frontier at a conference to commemorate the centennial of Turner's frontier thesis, I turned not to Turner himself, but returned instead to his better-known contemporary.[7]

Born in Portage, Wisconsin on November 14, 1861, Turner was roughly five years older than Laura Elizabeth Ingalls, who arrived February 7, 1867, in nearby Pepin. My effort to link Turner's Portage with Wilder's Pepin drew from the work of other scholars who probed the differences between the real Ingalls family and the fictional characters with the same names; between the ways the actual family history was pruned to emphasize conservative values and to construct images of frontier independence.[8] Tailored to a particular version of the Turnerian frontier, the Little House books also stretch its boundaries, particularly from the perspectives of gender, families, and the significance of private experience. Wilder's story introduces particular tensions between family-centered and state-centered narratives that illuminate what does change when we add "the feminine role" to frontier history.

No one articulated more clearly than Turner himself how we reinterpret the past. There are "no standard ultimate histories," he insisted. And, in probably his second-most-quoted passage, *"Each age writes the history of the past anew with reference to the conditions uppermost in its own time."* "By unconscious inheritance," he wrote in 1891, "and by conscious striving after the past as part of the present, history has acquired continuity."[9]

Part of Turner's own unconscious inheritance shaped a historical narrative without women. I intend no disrespect for Dr. Turner, a man who was, for his time, progressive. He also, like many men of his time and training, could not see women as agents of history, and therefore omitted them from his powerful narrative of national history that defined what made us Americans. The only woman who appears in "The Significance of the Frontier in American History," is Kit Carson's mother, and then only because she was related to Daniel Boone. That omission underscores the significance of gender in the Little House books, and the questions they may raise from a current vantage point.

For Turner, and for subsequent generations of American schoolchildren, American history began when Europeans landed on the eastern edge of the continent. National progress then moved in a direction—to the West. The story of westward expansion became the story of the country; western frontiers became the crucibles of American individualism and democracy.

Just as Turner revised the version of history he inherited, so subsequent generations revisited and reinterpreted the significance of his frontier. By the 1950s, consensus historians rejected the idea that the frontier created lasting changes in American values or institutions. In an era dominated by images of "Gunsmoke," "Westward Ho the Wagons," and "Davy Crockett," they focused on continuities between East and West and the unifying cultural power of a mythic and symbolic frontier.[10]

Many historians now challenge the idea that there was in fact a single pioneer experience. New Western Historians, influenced by the social movements of the past quarter century, have again reinterpreted the frontier from the perspectives of race, gender, environment, and conquest.[11] Emphasizing the varieties of pioneer experience in a region that was, from 1860-1900, the most ethnically diverse in the nation, they challenge Turner's assertion that "the frontier promoted the formation of a composite nationality for the American people."[12]

Throughout the nineteenth century, the U.S. as a nation moved West. But settlers arrived from many routes—from Norway, Sweden, and Russia, from China, Mexico, and Canada, as well as from the eastern U.S. "In the crucible of the frontier," Turner asserted, "the immigrants were Americanized, liberated and fused into a mixed race, English in neither nationality or characteristics."[13] His narrative of westward movement separated Americans from their immigrant roots by providing a single story from which to construct a new common national identity. New western histories, by contrast, explore the diverse identities and experiences of the women and men, immigrants and indigenous peoples who settled the American West.

The Little House books spoke powerfully to many readers in these continuing conversations between past and present. In her fiction, Laura Ingalls Wilder interpreted her pioneer childhood through the filters of her own memory, the historical contexts in which she wrote, and the conservative values she shared with her daughter-collaborator, Rose Wilder Lane. Lane participated in this interpretive enterprise not only as her mother's collaborator, but also as an author in her own right as she drew from her parents' histories to craft her own fiction. *Let the Hurricane Roar*, based on Ingalls family stories, and *Free Land*, based on her father's experiences, added the perspectives of the post-pioneer generation.[14] The Little House books, and the lives on which they drew, have, like Turner's frontier narrative, been continually reinterpreted—by readers, through the "Little House on the Prairie" television series, and by the continued production of new fictions based on the lives of various extended Ingalls and Wilder family members.

How then, did these versions of the frontier compare with Turner's? Turner's frontiers—the dividing lines between "savagery and civilization"—belonged sequentially to Indian traders, hunters, soldiers, ranchers, miners, and farmers.[15] Each economic stage defined a more advanced stage of human development. Men's jobs defined these frontiers. There was no school teachers' or missionaries' frontier, no laundry workers' frontier, no butter churners' frontier, and no chicken raisers' frontier.[16]

Three lines defined the forward progress of history in this triumphal western story. The first line moved from East to West. As the nation
moved West, human society, in an equally linear fashion, improved. The
second line moved upward from savagery to civilization, as white Americans conquered the wilderness and the indigenous people who lived there.
History progressed, Turner explained, as "primitive peoples" became "new
nations." Americans brought a superior civilization to "savages" whose
lives would be improved by adopting nuclear families, private property,
and Christianity. The third line of progress, to which we will return shortly,
charted the movement of social organization from families into states.[17]

A number of scholars have documented Laura Ingalls Wilder's
identification with the frontier, and have explored how she crafted her
own story to fit an inherited version of frontier history. The details of
daily survival could embellish any number of possible plots. It is the particular *plots* of fiction and history that I want to explore—the crafting of
narratives with chosen beginnings, endings, action, and themes.

The combined themes of family, maturation, and the frontier create particular tensions within the Little House narrative, between Laura
Ingalls' actual and fictional childhoods, and between Wilder's plot and
Turner's. Comparing Wilder's unpublished autobiography, "Pioneer Girl,"
written by 1930 for an adult audience, with the version in the Little House
books, we can chart what changed in the two accounts. Wilder deleted
portions of the Ingalls family migrations, omitted kin and neighbors, and
erased periods of extreme hardship, loss, and wage work, to craft the
family saga into a narrative of inexorable westward movement and gradual
maturation, to emphasize self-sufficiency rather than communal interdependence, and to suggest the ultimate triumph over obstacles and adversity that characterized Turnerian frontier history.[18] "Pioneer Girl" begins
with the Ingalls family's sojourn in Indian Territory, then traces the family's
migrations back to Pepin because government troops "were driving all the
white people off the Indians' land"; their return to Wisconsin ("the place
where we had left when we went west") because the man who bought the
land from Charles Ingalls "had not paid for it"; to a farm on Plum Creek
near Walnut Grove, Minnesota; to Burr Oak, Iowa; back to Walnut Grove;
and eventually to the future site of De Smet, South Dakota. It ends happily when the constant journeys stop, as Laura marries Almanzo Wilder.
Wilder concluded, "I was a little awed by my new estate, but I felt very
much at home and very happy, and among the other causes for happiness
was the thought that I would never again have to go and live with strangers in their houses. I had a house and a home of my own."[19]

Wilder's investment in a secure home of her own is etched in the foreground of constant movement, poverty, and childhood labor. She and Mary washed dishes and helped wait on table at the Burr Oak hotel, and took care of "Mrs. Steadman's baby Tommy all day Saturdays and Sundays." In Walnut Grove, she earned fifty cents a week at the Masters' hotel, where she "washed dishes and swept and dusted and made beds," cared for a baby, set the table and waited table. She went away "from home a good many days . . . helping Mrs. Goff on Saturdays and holidays" and left school to stay with Sadie Hurley on her farm. Her "Pioneer Girl" work record begins to resemble the Little House story only when the Ingallses reach Silver Lake, where Laura cooked and washed for hordes of settlers during the spring land rush in a house that "was always full of strangers." Later, she sewed for twenty-five cents a day for a local merchant's mother-in-law, because, she wrote, "we needed money" and worked again at her "old trade, taking care of babies so their mothers could go out in the evenings." She chronicles, too, the wage work that she wrote into *Little Town on the Prairie* and *These Happy Golden Years*: staying with Mrs. McKee on her homestead near Manchester; sewing for town milliner and dress-maker Florence Bell for fifty cents a day; and teaching three terms of school, two of which required her to live away from home.[20] In the Little House books however, her entry into the work world comes later and is a gradual part of growing up. In the more realistic "Pioneer Girl," working for strangers is a constant and often frightening element of an impoverished childhood. At a very young age, Laura heard about sex, domestic violence, and alcohol abuse, and feared that she would have to be adopted by another family to alleviate the family poverty in Burr Oak.[21]

In contrast to the back-and-forth migrations and recurring periods of hardship of the "Pioneer Girl" narrative, the Little House books are instead crafted to fit a combined plot of westward movement and Laura's gradual maturation from the warm security of childhood to an increasingly responsible and independent adolescence. The story begins, of course, in the Big Woods of Wisconsin, and erases the moves eastward to Pepin and Burr Oak in order to create a constant westward movement consonant with the inexorable migrations of Manifest Destiny. The happy endings are similar, but the fictional conclusion suggests not just settling but the triumph over adversity and the promise of increasing prosperity as the next generation, backed by a secure homestead, begins the saga anew amid the youthful saplings on Almanzo's tree claim.[22]

Laura Ingalls Wilder evidently knew and identified with the Turnerian narrative. In 1937 she declared that she had "seen the whole frontier, the woods, the Indian country of the great plains, the frontier towns, the building of the railroads in wild unsettled country, homesteading and farmers coming in to take possession. I realized," she said:

> that I had seen and lived it all—all the successive phases of the frontier, first the frontiersman then the pioneer, then the farmers and the towns.
> Then I understood that in my own life I represented a whole period of American history. That the frontier was gone and agricultura-settlements had taken its place when I married a farmer.[23]

Wilder's words echo Turner's repetitive pattern of waves of settlement. "Stand at Cumberland Gap," he wrote:

> and watch the procession of civilization, marching single file—the buffalo, following the trail to the salt springs, the Indian, the fur trader and hunter, the cattle raiser, the pioneer farmer—and the frontier has passed by. Stand at South Pass in the Rockies a century later, and see the same procession with wider intervals between.[24]

Wilder dated the end of the frontier at approximately the same time as Turner. He followed the Superintendent of the Census, who declared that the frontier had ended by 1890, when there was no longer an unbroken line of settlement with two or fewer settlers per square mile. Turner wrote his thesis to interpret an era he assumed was over. "And now," he concluded, "four centuries from the discovery of America, at the end of a hundred years of life under the Constitution, the frontier has gone, and with its going has closed the first period of American history."[25] The 1890 endpoint corresponds with Wilder's more personal periodization. She dated the close of the frontier from her 1885 marriage to Almanzo Wilder, midway between the 1880 and 1890 censuses which established for the government the time when there was still a frontier and when it had closed.

These similarities suggest that Wilder and Lane had absorbed a standard version of frontier history and used it (by unconscious inheritance or conscious striving) to make sense of their pioneer past. I am equally intrigued, however, with how Turner and Wilder diverge, and what their differences suggest about frontiers and gender.

They obviously diverged concerning the positive value Turner attached to free land, a concept that Rose Wilder Lane attacked in her novel *Free Land*, based on her father's pioneer experience, and their different judgments of the role of government. The ideological differences between Turner's progressive faith and Wilder's and Lane's conservative distrust of government are located partly in the historical circumstances in which they wrote.

Both narratives were conceived during times of extreme economic distress. In 1893, as Turner crafted "The Significance of the Frontier," the nation entered a devastating four-year depression. The collective response to adversity spawned the Populist Party and Coxey's Armies of the unemployed who marched eastward to Washington to demand relief in the form of government employment on massive public works projects. Coxey failed. But two young politicians heeded Turner's implicit message that American democracy required economic expansion. Theodore Roosevelt and Woodrow Wilson were both influenced by Turner to pursue foreign resources and international markets to replace the expansive promise of free land. As Wilder and Lane wrote, the U.S. was again plunged into a devastating depression. Again, the debate centered on the proper role of government in providing for collective relief. This time, however, the nation turned inward, away from an international arena that seemed as economically bleak as our own. The political debate, in literature as well as in Washington, centered on two competing visions, one based in collectivity and interdependence, the other in individualism, self-sufficiency, and self-reliance.

Or maybe not quite.

Because the national image of self-reliance, like the version we find in the Little House books, was based not on the isolated individual, but in the nuclear family. Rather than turning to the government, labor unions, or other collective politics, the self-reliant family could survive all difficulties, particularly with strong maternal women to pull their families through hard times. The nation turned from the youthful exuberance of the carefree flapper to the maternal solidity of Ma Joad.

And Laura Ingalls Wilder returned to her idealized childhood to teach the lessons she felt Americans desperately needed to understand in order to know what "made America as they know it."[26] Her reliance on the family inverted the final, least clearly elaborated, trajectory in Turner's model of frontier progress. The third line of progress in Turner's history assumed that public life was more important, historically, than private life. History progressed, Turner said, as people moved from families into states. In a famous passage in which he outlined the importance of the frontier in promoting democracy and individualism, Turner made passing reference to the pioneer family. "Complex society," he wrote, "is precipitated by the wilderness into a kind of primitive organization based on the family." Unlike

Lane and Wilder, who placed their faith in the family and insisted on minimal government interference, Turner did not dwell on this "primitive organization," nor did he see it as a positive seedbed of American values. "The tendency," he said, "is anti-social. It produces antipathy to control and particularly to any direct control..." He decried an ethic which confused "individual liberty ...with absence of all effective government."[27] History then progressed as men formed territories and governments, as they established states—the real subjects of history.[28]

Family households—those "primitive" social units—buried women in a history of the nation in which they were largely invisible. To see women, children, and families we must abandon the model of history that many of us absorbed in school—the unspoken assumption that history is about nations and that private life is subordinate to the public world of war and politics.

Wilder, by contrast, while affirming patriotic values, subordinated her extended family, the larger community, and the state to the nuclear family itself. Many of the differences between the lives and the stories tailor the Ingallses more clearly into self-reliant, independent pioneers. Ma and Pa are much more isolated in their fictional Little House, much closer to the primitive self-sufficiency Turner described, than Charles and Caroline's actual, typical experience of cooperative extended family settlement. They settled near Pepin surrounded by Charles's parents, numerous Ingalls and Quiner siblings, and other neighbors. In the story, their relatives are remote—mostly somewhere far away in the Big Woods.

No one else is there at all. Modoc writer and educator Michael Dorris wrote about his own experience when "with the enthusiasm of a father who had long looked forward to sharing a favorite tale" he began reading the *Little House in the Big Woods* to his two young daughters. On the first page he heard himself read: "As far as a man could go to the north in a day, or a week, or a whole month, there was nothing but woods. There were no houses. There were no roads. There were no people. There were only trees and the wild animals who had their homes among them." "Say what?" says Dorris.

Excuse me, but weren't we forgetting the Chippewa branch of my daughters' immediate ancestry, not to mention the thousands of resident Menominees, Potawatomis, Sauks, Foxes, Winnebagos, and Ottawas who inhabited mid-nineteenth-century Wisconsin. . . . Exactly upon whose indigenous land was Grandma and Grandpa's snug little house constructed? . . . This cozy, fun-filled world of extended Ingallses was curiously empty, a pristine wilderness in which only white folks toiled and cavorted, ate and harvested, celebrated and were kind to each other.[29]

Similarly, the other settlers who left Indian Territory with the family are crossed out of an early draft of "Pioneer Girl," along with the extended combined Ingalls and Quiner families who lived near the Pepin farm, the neighbors in the Big Woods, Walter Ogden who wintered with the family at Silver Lake, George and Maggie Masters who lived with the family during the Hard Winter, and anyone else who might clutter the story and turn it into a common frontier tale of extended family settlement and communal interdependence.[30]

The ways that Wilder crafted her story around the twin themes of Manifest Destiny and growing up create particular tensions in the narrative between Pa's masculine urge to wander to the next frontier (with which Laura identifies) and Ma's desire to settle, civilize, and enclose.[31] It created strains, too, between the idealized freedom and security of childhood and the restrictions of adulthood. The resolution was achieved partly through the chosen ending of *These Happy Golden Years* which "ends happily," Wilder said, "as all good novels should when Laura of the Little Houses and Almanzo of *Farmer Boy* were married."[32] That ending neatly combined the conventions of romance, in which a long foreground of waiting ends when a young girl meets her Prince Charming and rides with him into the sunset, and the mythologized ending of the frontier, when the elbow room is gone, the frontier is closed, and the hero rides off to begin again. But if the ending resolved certain tensions in the novel, it did not resolve them in ways consistent with the lived experiences of the Ingalls and Wilder families, or with the actual experiences of many of their pioneer contemporaries. To understand the limits of both Wilder's plot and Turner's, we must confront the differences between the real and fictional childhoods, between idealized self-sufficiency and real dependence and interdependence, between the fictional happy ending and what really happened next. The point is not so much the contrast between real lives and fiction, as how those differences illuminate the interpretations of pioneer experience in a collective history.

Although Pa and Ma both affirm the value of a self-reliant nuclear family, Pa represents the continued urge to re-capture the "primitive organization" of an isolated nuclear family, while Ma speaks for the value of neighbors, community, and civilized institutions. When Laura shares Pa's constant desire to move on to the next frontier, she creates a conflict for herself by gendering the frontier as masculine and the post-frontier community as feminine. Throughout, it is Pa who wants to leave when the neighborhood gets too crowded, Ma who values schools, churches, kin, and other women's company.[33] In the contexts of real life, we can understand both Caroline's urge to stay, and Charles's urge to move to Oregon in 1879, after the grasshoppers destroyed his wheat crops and forced him into five years of wage labor. These terrible years included the death of the Ingallses' son and left Caroline and Charles, at forty and forty-three, landless, poor, and struggling to support four children from two to fourteen, the oldest of whom was blind.[34]

Erasing these years helps fit the Ingallses into the pioneer myth. The difficult years of loss, failure, moving East and living in town are omitted, so that the family can overcome adversity in its constant journey West and help re-create "complex society" in De Smet. But these erasures also make it more difficult to explain how each move is an improvement for the family, and they make it difficult for Laura, who loves the frontier, to want to grow up.

Although Wilder's actual childhood included considerable poverty, enclosure, and labor, not until the fictional Laura is fifteen does she work outside her home or encounter the world of sex and courtship. As *Little Town on the Prairie* opens, Laura must leave springtime on the homestead claim and begin to work in town as a seamstress to help the family send Mary to attend the college for the blind in Iowa.

> "One evening at supper, Pa asked, 'How would you like to work in town, Laura?'...
> "A job? For a girl? In town?" Ma said. "Why, what kind of a job—" Then quickly she said, "No, Charles, I won't have Laura working out in a hotel among all kinds of strangers."
> "Who said such a thing?" Pa demanded. "No girl of ours'll do that, not while I'm alive and kicking."
> "Of course not," Ma apologized. "You took me so by surprise. What other kind of work can there be? and Laura not old enough to teach school yet."[35]

There is, of course, considerable irony here for the little girl who began to work at age nine in the Burr Oak Hotel. But she didn't write it. This is one of the "framing" chapters that Rose Wilder Lane added as she edited her mother's work.[36]

Both the real Laura and her character worked so that Mary could attend the Iowa College for the Blind in Vinton, Iowa, where Charles and Caroline enrolled her in November 1881. But again the story was slightly altered. Wilder wrote in her original draft:

> Dakota Territory still had no school where the blind could be
> educated, but the territory would pay tuition, to the state of Iowa, for all
> Dakota blind children. And Mary could go to the Iowa College for the
> blind at Vinton. Tuition included board and room and books.
>   With all this taken care of, there would be left the expense of
> the new clothes Mary must have and the railroad fare to Vinton. Mary
> must have some spending money. . . .[37]

Rose Wilder Lane deleted this part so that the independent
Ingallses would not have to take a government subsidy. The significance
of whose story we're getting gets clearer in its complexity if we examine
Lane's own version.

In 1933, a year after the first *Little House in the Big Woods* appeared, Lane published her own fictional version of her grandparents' pioneer saga. In *Let the Hurricane Roar* a young pioneer couple, Charles
and Caroline, marry and move West together to find land. This Charles
and Caroline have known each other since their childhoods in the Big
Woods. Charles is a fiddler. Caroline is a quiet person: "all her movements were gentle and deft." They move West; he works as a teamster on
the railroad; Caroline becomes pregnant. They settle in a dugout on the
banks of Wild Plum Creek. After a horrendous but distantly rendered
labor, young Charles John is born. Charles borrows against a promising
wheat crop. But grasshoppers eat the wheat, and Charles must go East to
work as a harvest hand. And here we encounter a more romantic and
polarized version of pioneer femininity and masculinity. Caroline lets him
go because: "He must not lose his pride; it was their most precious possession." "She marveled that a man's pride was so essential to him that he
could not let it go, and be content with love. But that was true."

> Only a defeated man traveled eastward, homeless, with a wife and
> little baby. All day long poor little Charles John, hot and tired and wail-
> ing, would be jolting in the wagon. All the way Charles would know,
> and every man he met would know, that he hadn't been strong enough
> for the West.[38]

Caroline struggles alone in the dugout with the baby through a
hard winter of continuous blizzards, until Charles returns to her in mid-
blizzard with $40 to show for his labors. And this Caroline knows that
they will triumph over adversity to achieve prosperity on their own land.

Somehow, without quite thinking it, she felt that light from the future was shining in the baby's face. The big white house was waiting for him, and the acres of wheat fields, the fast driving teams and swift buggies. If he remembered at all this life in the dugout, he would think of it only as a brief prelude to more spacious times.[39]

And that is the problem with the fictional versions of these lives, and with a history that romanticized the complex lives of actual pioneers. The little houses were not in fact, for these and many other pioneer families, the brief preludes to more spacious times.

The story did not end, of course, with the Ingallses and Wilders cozily settled on their homesteads, secure against ever again having "to live with strangers," as Wilder ended the story of her pioneer girl. For Laura and Almanzo, Rose's difficult birth in 1886 left a debt to the doctor; a bout with diphtheria left Almanzo lame; the Wilders' newborn son died in 1889; their first home on his tree claim burned; they lost the homestead claim. Drought destroyed their crops and killed the trees on Almanzo's tree claim, forcing him into debt and pre-emption. The dismal details of loss parallel the experiences of many victims of drought and depression in the 1890s and 1930s alike.

Wilder drafted the story of these years in the early 1930s, a tale she called "The First Three Years and a Year of Grace." She intended it as an adult novel, or as material for Rose 's work. Rose Wilder Lane never touched it. When Lane's executor, Roger Lea MacBride, published it in 1971, *The First Four Years* pried chinks between Laura's version of her life and the collaborative fiction.[40] This Laura, for instance, does not want to marry a farmer "because a farm is such a hard place for a woman. There are so many chores for her to do, and harvest help and threshers to cook for. Besides a farmer never has any money." Although Wilder forced an upbeat ending to the onslaught of disasters, she and her husband lost everything.[41] Leaving De Smet in 1890, they stayed awhile with his parents in Spring Valley, Minnesota, then moved briefly to Florida. Returning to De Smet, they worked there from 1892-94 to save enough to leave for good. Finally, over the next two decades, they built their Rocky Ridge Farm near Mansfield in southern Missouri. They did not "succeed" until Rose had left home and they were well into middle age.[42]

The Ingalls family lived on their homestead through 1887. Charles Ingalls "proved up" on his claim on December 20, 1888, but drought discouraged farming. Caroline owned two lots on Third Street in De Smet. Charles built a house there; they moved in on Christmas Eve, 1887, and never left again. Caroline sometimes kept boarders. Charles worked as a carpenter, held a number of town offices, sold insurance and binding twine. He opened a general store in 1892, but it soon folded in the dismal economy. Charles died in 1902. Caroline remained on Third Street with Mary, subsisting on boarders and help from Carrie and Grace. She died in 1924.[43]

Do the differences between these endings and the fictional one matter? The answer depends on how we connect the past with the present. Turner again: "No age has suffered the highest content of the past to be lost entirely. By unconscious inheritance and by conscious striving after the past as part of the present, history has acquired continuity." What we make of these stories and the lives they represent depends on how we conceive the "highest content" of our pioneer pasts, how we judge the values of family and community, independence and cooperation, democracy and inequality that different Americans read into these experiences.

The mythic frontier of western opportunity required that long years of struggle be redeemed when the pioneers could live securely ever after on their hard-won homesteads. The next stage is supposed to be the agricultural settlements with which Wilder defined the end of her own frontier saga. But most homesteaders did not succeed; the majority did not prove up and gain title to their land. For the minority who made it, many considered homesteading an investment in a non-agricultural future. The land might provide a stake for a business, for education, or some other goal.[44] In an era in which farming increasingly meant production for markets, the family farm was threatened and the larger migration was not from East to West but from farm to city. The details of the Ingalls family history might more easily fit that plot than the frontier saga. The details of domestic labor in the Little House books that so vividly drew me to pioneer women *could* be used to chronicle the industrial transformation of women's work, by tracing, for instance, the changes from Almanzo's mother's spinning thread and weaving cloth in the 1850s to Ma's crafting garments with store-bought fabric on her treasured sewing machine in the 1880s. Similarly, we could chart the move from a family economy that rested on hunting, farming, and domestic food preservation in the Big Woods, to the farm on the banks of Plum Creek where Charles intended to raise wheat for the St. Paul flour mills. The railroad tied Minnesota and South Dakota farmers to distant markets, and set up the dependencies for fuel, flour, and processed foods that are evident from *The Long Winter* forward.

The inevitable confrontations with this new and uncertain adult world are compounded by gender in Laura's and Almanzo's fictional childhoods. The particular issues of the "feminine role" catalyze when Laura must leave childhood security for the challenges of an adult pioneer woman. This becomes problematic because the fictional childhood security sets up a story of material decline rather than progressive prosperity, and because as she grows up she must renounce the masculine frontier to enter Ma's more restricted domestic world. This is not a problem for Almanzo on the prosperous Wilder farm of *Farmer Boy*. Almanzo, a growing boy with a hefty workload, seems to have two major preoccupations—getting a colt and eating a lot. Consider one meal:

> Almanzo ate the sweet, mellow baked beans. He ate the bit of salt pork that melted like cream in his mouth. He ate mealy boiled potatoes, with brown ham-gravy. He ate the ham. He bit deep into velvety bread spread with sleek butter, and he ate the crisp golden crust. He demolished a tall heap of pale mashed turnips, and a hill of stewed yellow pumpkin. Then he sighed, and tucked his napkin deeper into the neckband of his red waist. And he ate plum preserves, and strawberry jam, and grape jelly, and spiced watermelon-rind pickles. He felt very comfortable inside. Slowly he ate a large piece of pumpkin pie.

For an encore he consumes apples, popcorn, and cider by the stove after supper.[45]

Both Laura and Almanzo have abundant childhoods filled with a variety of homegrown foods. Both learn the skills they will need when they grow up. But Almanzo has choices. He rejects both his brother Royal's decision to become a storekeeper, and an apprenticeship offered by a friendly wagonmaker. Almanzo chooses farming, for a very simple reason. "I like horses," he tells Royal. When his father asks him what *he* wants, Almanzo pauses in mid-bite to reply, "I want a colt." When he is frustrated, he wonders if he will "ever be big enough to have anything he wanted. . . .He wanted to drive the horses, himself."[46] Almanzo's dream may take awhile, but he has choices, he says what he wants, and eventually he gets it.

In all eight volumes of his wife's novel, we learn little else about this oddly silent man. He works hard; he likes to eat; he likes horses. But he offers us a crucial contrast. Almanzo wants to grow up. Laura doesn't.

Laura's choices are narrower, more conflicted, and they come later. Her options seem typical enough for a frontier farm girl—sewing, teaching, or marriage. She either does not see or does not validate other options—the life of a single woman homesteader, for instance, represented by both her sister-in-law, Eliza Jane Wilder, and by her own sister, Carrie

Ingalls, or the perspectives of women who wanted to go back to the East.
She fears the woman who most completely rejects the supporting role of
pioneer wife. When Laura Ingalls taught her first school, she boarded
with a family named Bouchie who became, in *These Happy Golden Years*,
the fictional Brewster family—one of only two name changes Wilder made
in her books.⁴⁷ Mrs. Brewster, a sullen woman, does not want to be there.
The house is dirty, the baby squalls incessantly, and no one is remotely
pleasant. Laura awakens one night to see Mrs. Brewster threatening her
husband with a butcher knife to make him take her back East. "I've got
you and Johnny to support," he tells her, "and nothing in the world but this
claim. Go put up that knife and come to bed before you freeze."⁴⁸ Although Wilder reported a similar incident in "Pioneer Girl," the only apparent provocation was Mrs. Bouchie's insistence that her husband had kicked
her. Wilder wrote that "I never knew what she was furious about.... "⁴⁹
Certainly it is understandable that this violence horrified and frightened
the young Laura Ingalls, and that it might have fed her determination not
to have to live again among strangers. But of all the violent scenes that
Laura Ingalls Wilder edited out of "Pioneer Girl," she preserved this one,
and invented a motivation that vilified the woman who rejected life on an
isolated homestead. Wilder steadfastly rejected any backsliding from the
frontier ideal. "No one that I heard of," she insisted, "ever thought of
leaving and going back east."⁵⁰

She did allow the fictional Laura to resist growing up to adult
constraints. Mary had wanted to teach school. "Laura did not want to,
but now she must; she had to be able to teach school as soon as she grew
old enough, to earn money for Mary's college education."⁵¹ She hates her
new corsets which are "a sad affliction to her..."Ma and Mary wear their
corsets at night, but Laura could not bear at night the torment of the steels
that would not let her draw a deep breath."⁵² Wilder reported more pro-
saically in "Pioneer Girl," "though I had begun wearing corsets when I
was fourteen, I would not wear them except when I was dressed up, and
then would not lace them in as Ma thought I should, to have a pretty
waist."⁵³

When Laura resists proper womanhood, it is because she is western. This is symbolized throughout by her refusal to wear her sunbonnet,
despite Ma's warning that she will become "brown as an Indian." Nellie
Oleson, Laura's childhood nemesis who prefers town to country, and East
to West, refuses to join Laura and her friends outdoors. "My goodness,
no!" she exclaims. "Why, this wind will tan your skin!" "...In the East, a
lady always keeps her skin white and her hands smooth."⁵⁴

Laura's task, as she matures, is to reconcile womanhood with the frontier. Her resolution lies in the family, and in the progress of American history.

I take my text from *Little Town on the Prairie.*

> It is Friday night. "As usual, Laura opened her history book."
> Suddenly she could not bear it all. She thrust back her chair, slammed her book shut and thumped it down on the table. Pa and Ma started, and looked at her in surprise.
> "I don't care!" she cried out. "I don't want to study! I don't want to learn! I don't want to teach school, *ever!*"
> Ma looked as stern as it was possible for her to look. *"Laura,"* she said, "I know you would not swear, but losing your temper and slamming things is as bad as saying the words. Let us have no more wooden swearing."
> Laura did not answer.
> "What is the matter, Laura?" Pa asked. "Why don't you want to learn, and to teach school?"
> "Oh, I don't know!" Laura said in despair. "I am so tired of everything. I want—I want something to happen. I want to go West. I guess I want to just play, and I know I am too old," she almost sobbed, a thing she never did.
> "Why, Laura!" Ma exclaimed.

Ma suggests that "for this one evening" she put her books away and read aloud a story from the last bundle of *Youth's Companion.* "Yes, Ma," Laura replies hopelessly. But "Even reading a story was not what she wanted. She did not know what she wanted, but she knew she could not have it, whatever it was."[55]

Pa's solution is better. He organizes a town spelling bee. He gets her out of the house.

It is finally a combination of school, church, and history that propel Laura into the womanhood for which Ma prepares her.

Almanzo Wilder walks her home from church.

She is chosen to recite the first half of American history at the School Exhibition. "America was discovered by Christopher Columbus in 1492," she begins, then plows through the Spanish and French explorers, Raleigh, and the English and Dutch settlements.

As she speaks, "Pa's face stands out from all the others. His eyes met hers and they were shining as he slowly nodded his head."

Then Laura was "really launched upon the great history of America. She told of the vision of freedom and equality in the New World, and she told of the old oppressions of Europe. . . ." She recites the accomplishments of each President. Under Washington there is "the opening of the Northwest Territory." She skips lightly over Adams (who acquired no new territory), to Jefferson who "bought for the new country all the land between the Mississippi and California," to Jackson who "went down from Tennessee and fought the Spanish and took Florida," to John Quincy Adams. "So down from the Missouri went the Santa Fe traders, across a thousand miles of desert, to trade with Mexico. Then the first wagon wheels rolled into Kansas." She finishes to thunderous applause, and finds herself looking "up into the face of Almanzo Wilder."[56]

Manifest Destiny strikes again. But he walks her right back home.

The fact that there were no Ingalls sons allowed Laura to enter her father's world, but only for a time. And that's the problem. She must stop wanting to wander West, stop wanting to play. She must grow up to stay put and go back into the "primitive organization" of her Little House. This brings us back to the original dilemma—we can't simply add a "feminine role" to Turner's frontier, because the "feminine role" is to settle and civilize. Women's stories take us past the frontier, past the adventure, past childhood, past the fun.

Who, in these stories, would want to grow up? The childhood larders are full of food. Almanzo feels very comfortable inside. Why would anyone want to leave these warm, secure places? But the neighbors always arrive, the game always leaves, they always move West, and become more dependent. The abundant self-sufficiency of the Big Woods declines to dependent near-starvation by the Long Winter, when the railroad is blocked. Even in good times, the Ingallses' diet often contracts to salt pork and bread made with store-bought flour. As Laura moves West and grows up, she encounters dependence—on railroads, on agricultural markets, on neighbors.

To be sure, the Ingallses do get their homestead, and Laura and Almanzo settle on their tree claim.

But that's as far as we can go. Almanzo *will* travel eastward "a defeated man . . . homeless, with a wife and little [girl]." Did he believe, did Rose or Laura believe "that he hadn't been strong enough for the West"? How did his wife judge him or judge herself because they "thought of leaving and going back east"? He later wrote his daughter, "My life has been mostly disappointments."[57] When Laura and Almanzo finally could move to their farm and complete the farmhouse, Almanzo was fifty-six, Laura was forty-six, and Rose, who had never lived there, was twenty-nine.

Finally, in these sagas of frontier gender, the figure we are least able to see is Almanzo. His story most violates the conventions of pioneer opportunity, which define manhood as they define national progress.

But was Charles Ingalls so very different? Charles and Caroline finally did settle in their house in De Smet. When they proved up their homestead, Charles was fifty-two; Caroline, forty-nine. The Ingallses' house was built on Caroline's lot; Laura earned the down payment for the Wilders' Missouri farm; $500 from Almanzo's father enabled them to finish the farmhouse.[58] Neither Charles nor Almanzo fit Rose's ideal prescriptions for independent pioneer manhood.

If we really enter the adult world, the gender polarities blur. Pa helps organize the church and school. Charles Ingalls was a devout Congregationalist, a civilizer who built Masonic lodges and churches, who served as a Justice of the Peace. Laura remembered him as a gentle nurturer. He stopped wandering when Caroline wouldn't go further. He was more androgynous and more tied to his girls than any Marlboro Man would like. The stories of real pioneers force us not just to add the feminine role, but to reassess stereotypes of the frontiersman as well.

Finally, we need to reconsider the romance that bathes these remembered childhoods. The warm glow of the Little House masks some childhoods of considerable pain, hunger, and uncertainty, perhaps considerable anger. Only a child who had been hungry could eat as much as Almanzo.[59]

The frontier myth can sustain hard times if they lead quickly to better things for the pioneers or their children. In these lives, they didn't. And so the story must end before Laura grows up, the characters move East, and the farmers move to town.

How might Caroline Ingalls have ended her own story? How would she have described the little houses of pioneer women—those primitive organizations where people were interdependent, neighbors were valued, and where family stories sometimes contradict a triumphal history of national progress? Caroline Ingalls' own life may have written the happy ending for her and many other pioneers—a house in town near a church, school, and neighbors.

If we really examined "the feminine role" it would turn the frontier outside in. It would shift our focus from the new nation to the family, with all its difficult legacies of intimacy, labor, interdependence, and endurance.

There is considerable hope in facing the limits of Turner's and Wilder's frontiers, of the mythic frontiers we have inherited. We might imagine histories that did not locate gains and losses unambiguously in either families or the state. By reconceiving frontiers through the lives of the people who cannot inhabit them we push the boundaries of what is historically possible—then and now. Turner's words provide a useful compass: to strive consciously for the past as part of the present we must identify and evaluate the unconscious inheritances that we bring to our history. Because it is not enough to be able to identify with the characters in our pioneer past, as I was able to identify as a child with the fictional little girl named Laura. The plots, to function as history, must be able to connect us to the adult worlds we inhabit, and to the present that we inherit. And it is fair and important, I think, as we revisit and reinvent a pioneer past, to ask ourselves whether we are imagining a collective childhood as we wish it had been, or one that explains the adults we are and might yet become.

Notes

I am grateful to Linda Biesele Hall, William Cronon, and Susan Armitage for their comments on earlier drafts. I am grateful, too, to the Herbert Hoover Presidential Library Association for supporting my research, and to the staff of the Herbert Hoover Presidential Library, particularly Dwight M. Miller, for making it easy and pleasant to work there.

Endnotes

1. Frederick Jackson Turner, "The Significance of the Frontier in American History," first presented at the Historical Congress in Chicago at the World's Columbian Exhibition of 1893, originally printed in *The Annual Report of the American Historical Association for the Year 1893* (Washington, D.C. Government Printing Office, 1894). Turner's essay is quoted here from *History, Frontier, and Section: Three Essays by Frederick Jackson Turner*, Martin Ridge, ed. (Albuquerque: University of New Mexico Press, 1993), 59-92.

2. George Wilson Pierson, "American Historians and the Frontier Hypothesis in 1941 (II)," in Lawrence O. Burnette, Jr., comp., *Wisconsin Witness to Frederick Jackson Turner: A Collection of Essays on the Historian and the Thesis* (Madison: The State Historical Society of Wisconsin, 1961), 149. Pierson's article, based on an informal report to the Mississippi Valley and American Historical Associations at their annual meeting in Chicago, December 30, 1941, was originally published in two parts, in the September and December, 1942 issues of *Wisconsin Magazine*.

3. David M. Potter, "American Women and the American Character," a lecture presented in 1959 at Stetson University, in Don E. Fehrenbacher, ed. *History and American Society: Essays of David M. Potter* (New York: Oxford University Press,

1973), 277-303.

4. Many scholars date the emergence of western women's history as a distinct field from the publication of Joan M. Jensen and Darlis A. Miller, "The Gentle Tamers Revisited: New Approaches to the History of Women in the American West," *Pacific Historical Review* 49:2 (May 1980): 173-213. For early works on the Euro-American frontier, see Julie Roy Jeffrey, *Frontier Women: The Trans-Mississippi West, 1840-1890* (New York: Hill and Wang, 1979), Sandra L. Myres, *Westering Women and the Frontier Experience, 1800-1915* (Albuquerque: University of New Mexico Press, 1982), and Glenda Riley, *Frontierswomen, The Iowa Experience* (Ames, Iowa: Iowa State University Press, 1981). For reviews of scholarship on western women, see Jensen and Miller, "Gentle Tamers Revisited," and Elizabeth Jameson, "Toward a Multicultural History of Women in the Western United States," *Signs* 13:4 (Summer 1988): 761-91. For a discussion of women's frontiers, see Elizabeth Jameson and Susan Armitage, eds., *Writing the Range: Race, Class, and Culture in the Women's West* (Norman: University of Oklahoma Press, 1997), esp. 9-10, 81-84.

5. Charles Elliott, review of *The First Four Years, Time*, March 15, 1971, 92.

6. In November 1993, HarperCollins, reported that over 35 million of the "Little House" books had sold since their publication. Telephone communication, HarperCollins, November 2, 1993.

7. Portions of this article were first presented at the conference, "Turner and His Frontiers: Legacies and Opportunities," Madison, Wisconsin, November 13, 1993. I am grateful to William Cronon who invited me to speak and encouraged this work in the early stages, and to David Myers, who helped make it all happen.

8. Wilder scholars owe a great deal to William T. Anderson's research on the Ingalls and Wilder families. See William T. Anderson, *The Story of the Ingalls* (revised ed., 1993; available through Laura Ingalls Wilder Memorial Society, De Smet, S. D.); *The Story of the Wilders* (1983 ed.; Davison, Michigan: Anderson Publications, 1983); *Laura's Rose: The Story of Rose Wilder Lane* (Centennial Edition; De Smet, S. D.: Laura Ingalls Wilder Memorial Society, 1986); *Laura Wilder of Mansfield* (1982 ed.; De Smet, S. D.: Laura Ingalls Wilder Memorial Society, 1982); ed., *A Wilder in the West: The Story of Eliza Jane Wilder* (De Smet, South Dakota: Laura Ingalls Wilder Memorial Society, 1971; 1985 ed.). "The Literary Apprenticeship of Laura Ingalls Wilder," *South Dakota History* 13 (1983): 285-331; 287-90 describes some of the early questioning of minor differences between the actual lives and the fictional accounts. Other scholarship that probed the differences between the lives and the Little House books, and the authorial relationship between Laura Ingalls Wilder and Rose Wilder Lane, includes Donald Zochert, *Laura: The Life of Laura Ingalls Wilder* (Chicago: Contemporary Books, Inc., 1976); William Holtz, *The Ghost in the Little House: A Life of Rose Wilder Lane* (Columbia: University of Missouri Press, 1993); Louise Hovde Mortensen, "Idea Inventory," *Elementary English* 41 (April 1964): 428; Rosa Ann Moore, "Laura Ingalls Wilder's Orange Notebooks and the Art of the Little House Books," in *Children's Literature*, vol. 4 (Philadelphia: Temple University Press,

1975), 105-19; "Laura Ingalls Wilder and Rose Wilder Lane: The Chemistry of Collaboration," *Children's Literature in Education* (Autumn 1980): 101-9; "The Little House Books: Rose-Colored Classics," *Children's Literature* 7 (1978): 7-16; Anita Clair Fellman, "Laura Ingalls Wilder and Rose Wilder Lane: The Politics of a Mother-Daughter Relationship," *Signs: Journal of Women in Culture and Society* 13:3 (1990): 535-61; "Everybody's 'Little Houses': Reviewers and Critics Read Laura Ingalls Wilder," *Publishing Research Quarterly* 12:1 (Spring 1996): 3-19; "'Don't Expect to Depend on Anybody Else': The Pioneer as Portrayed in the Little House Books," *Children's Literature* 24 (1996): 101-116; Ann Romines, "The Long Winter: An Introduction to Western Womanhood," *Great Plains Quarterly* 18:1 (Winter 1990): 36-47.

9. Frederick Jackson Turner, "The Significance of History," in Ridge, ed., *History, Frontier, and Section*, 46, 49. This essay was originally published in the *Wisconsin Journal of Education* in 1891.

10. See Earl Pomeroy, "Toward a Reorientation of Western History: Continuity and Environment," *Mississippi Valley Historical Review*, 41 (March 1955): 579-600; Henry Nash Smith, *Virgin Land: The American West as Symbol and Myth* (New York: Vintage Books, 1950).

11. The New Western History is a large, diverse, and vital field, which generates multiple interpretations and considerable internal debate. For representative works, see Patricia Nelson Limerick, *The Legacy of Conquest: The Unbroken Past of the American West* (New York: W. W. Norton & Company, 1987); Richard White, *It's Your Misfortune and None of My Own: A New History of the American West* (Norman: University of Oklahoma Press, 1991); Patricia Nelson Limerick, Clyde A, Milner II, and Charles Rankin, eds., *Trails: Toward a New Western History* (Lawrence: University Press of Kansas, 1991); and William Cronon, George Miles, and Jay Gitlin, eds., *Under an Open Sky* (New York: W. W. Norton & Company, 1992). For works that emphasize differences of race and gender, see Quintard Taylor, *In Search of the Racial Frontier: African Americans in the American West, 1528-1990* (New York: W.W. Norton & Company, 1998); William Loren Katz, *The Black West* (Garden City, New York: Anchor Press, 1973); George J. Sanchez, *Becoming Mexican American: Ethnicity, Culture and Identity in Chicano Los Angeles, 1900-1945* (New York: Oxford University Press, 1993); Roger Daniels, *Asian America: Chinese and Japanese in the United States Since 1850* (Seattle: University of Washington Press, 1950); Sucheng Chan, Douglas Henry Daniels, Mario T. Garcia, and Terry P. Wilson, eds., *Peoples of Color in the American West* (Lexington, Massachusetts: D.C. Heath and Company, 1994); Susan Armitage and Elizabeth Jameson, eds., *The Women's West* (Norman: University of Oklahoma Press, 1987); Richard White, *The Roots of Dependency: Subsistence, Environment, and Social Change among the Choctaws, Pawnees, and Navajos* (Lincoln: University of Nebraska Press, 1983); Jameson and Armitage, eds., *Writing the Range.*

12. Turner, "Significance of the Frontier," 75.

13. Ibid., 76.

14. Rose Wilder Lane, *Let the Hurricane Roar* (New York: Longmans, Green and Co., 1933); and Lane, *Free Land* (New York: Longmans, Green and Co., 1938).

15. Turner, "Significance of the Frontier," 60, 67.

16. William Cronon, Howard R. Lamar, Katherine G. Morrissey, and Jay Gitlin comment that women's work never became the basis for a frontier classification, that we do not speak of a "chicken frontier" as we do of a "cattle frontier," though there is no logical reason not to. See Cronon, et al, "Women and the West: Rethinking the Western History Survey Course," *Western Historical Quarterly* XVII: 3 (July 1986): 269-90, 272-73. It might be noted, then, that Wilder's literary career had its roots, in her writing for the *Missouri Ruralist*, quite literally on the "chicken frontier."

17. Turner, "Significance of the Frontier," 60, 67-75.

18. Laura Ingalls Wilder wrote her draft of "Pioneer Girl" between 1927-1930; Rose Wilder Lane typed several drafts and submitted them to agents. I am working here primarily from the typed manuscript of "Pioneer Girl" sent to Carl Brandt, Rose Wilder Lane Papers, Laura Ingalls Wilder Series, Herbert Hoover Presidential Library, West Branch, Iowa. All quotes refer to this manuscript unless otherwise noted.

19. Wilder, "Pioneer Girl," 6, 7, 160.

20. Ibid., 43, 51, 53, 87, 112-13, 123, 135-37, 125-32, 141, 156-57.

21. Ibid., 37-38; 52-6; 63-4; Revised Draft, pp. 35, 42; Manuscripts, Notes, & Resource Material, "Pioneer Girl" manuscript sent George T. Bye) 9-10, 59-60, 141-42.

22. Wilder considered the eight volumes a composite children's novel: *Little House in the Big Woods* (New York: Harper & Brothers Publishers, 1932); *Farmer Boy* (New York: Harper & Brothers Publishers, 1933); *Little House on the Prairie* (New York: Harper & Brothers Publishers, 1935); *On the Banks of Plum Creek* (New York: Harper & Brothers Publishers, 1937); *By the Shores of Silver Lake* (New York: Harper & Brothers Publishers, 1939); *The Long Winter* (New York: Harper & Brothers Publishers, 1940); *Little Town on the Prairie* (New York: Harper & Brothers Publishers, 1941); *These Happy Golden Years* (New York: Harper & Brothers Publishers, 1943). All citations in this article are from the uniform edition of the series, with new illustrations by Garth Williams (New York: Harper & Brothers Publishers, 1953).

23. Wilder, Bookweek Speech, Detroit, October, 1937, Rose Wilder Lane Papers, Laura Ingalls Wilder Series, Herbert Hoover Presidential Library, West Branch, Iowa, 3.

24. Turner, "Significance of the Frontier," 67.

25. Ibid., 88.

26. Wilder, Bookweek Speech, 3.

27. Turner, "Significance of the Frontier," 82.

28. Ibid., 60, 67-75.

29. Michael Dorris, "Trusting the Words," *Booklist* (June 1 & 15, 1993): 1820-22.

30. See "Pioneer Girl," 6, 62, 94-6, 101.

31. The common stereotype of western women as civilizers is analyzed in Beverly Stoeltje, "A Helpmate for Man Indeed: The Image of the Frontier Woman," *Journal of American Folklore* 88:347 (Jan.-March 1975): 27-31.

32. Wilder, Bookweek Speech, 8.

33. See, for instance, *By the Shores of Silver Lake*, 195-96.

34. Anderson, *Story of the Ingalls*, 8.

35. Wilder, *Little Town on the Prairie*, 1-2.

36. For the original texts of Wilder's manuscript, and Lane's introductory chapters, see Holtz, *Ghost in the Little House*, 380-82.

37. Ibid., 384. This version is quoted from the manuscript of *Little Town on the Prairie*. A slightly different version appears in "Pioneer Girl," copy sent to Bye, 142: "For a long time we had been hoping to send Mary to a college for the blind. We had learned of such a college, at Vinton, Iowa. It was the Iowa State College for the Blind, intended only for Iowans, but we could send Mary there by paying tuition and board." See also Anderson, *Story of the Ingalls*, 14-15.

38. Lane, *Let the Hurricane Roar*, quotes, 3, 5, 77-79

39. Ibid., 152.

40. Wilder, *The First Four Years* (New York: Harper & Row, Publishers, 1971). Anderson, "Literary Apprenticeship," 292-99, makes the case that the manuscript was drafted between 1933 and 1937, rather than after *These Happy Golden Years*, shortly before Almanzo Wilder died in 1949, as Rose Wilder Lane's executor, Roger Lea MacBride, guessed in his introduction to *The First Four Years*, xiv. On differences between the two books, see for instance Janet Spaeth, *Laura Ingalls Wilder* (Boston: Twayne Publishers, 1987), 68-71.

41. Ibid., 3-4.

42. On the difficult years in Missouri before the Wilders were able to complete Rocky Ridge Farm and move to their house there, see Anderson, *Laura Wilder of Mansfield*; Wilder, *On the Way Home: The Diary of a Trip from South Dakota to Mansfield, Missouri, in 1894* (New York: Harper & Row, Publishers, 1962); Holtz, *Ghost in the Little House*, 29-46; Anderson, *Story of the Wilders*, 22-28; *Laura's Rose*, 7-13; and *Laura Ingalls Wilder: A Biography* (New York: HarperCollins Publishers, 1992), 143-81.

43. Anderson, *Story of the Ingalls*, 15-27. It is not clear how Caroline Ingalls bought the lots, or why they were entered in her name alone. Nor is it clear why Charles Ingalls waited longer than the required five years to "prove up" his homestead claim.

44. For data on single women homesteaders in North Dakota, including success rates in "proving up" and gaining title to claims, comparisons in the success rates of women and men, and how women used their land or disposed of it after gaining title, see H. Elaine Lindgren, *Land in Her Own Name: Single Women as Homesteaders in North Dakota* (Norman: University of Oklahoma Press, 1996).

45. Wilder, *Farmer Boy*, 28-29, 33. Spaeth, *Laura Ingalls Wilder*, 59-67, also emphasizes eating, growing up, and Almanzo's desire for horses.

46. Wilder, *Farmer Boy*, 297, 369, 92.

47. The other was her nemesis, Nellie Oleson, and her family. She based the character on Nellie Owens, the daughter of a Walnut Grove storekeeper, who had a brother named Willie, as did the fictional Nellie Oleson. The fictional Nellie is a composite of Nellie Owens and Genevieve Masters, daughter of Walnut Grove schoolteacher Sam Masters, whose family also followed the Ingallses to De Smet. See Anderson, *Laura Ingalls Wilder*, 53-4, 78, 80-81, 110-11.

48. Wilder, *These Happy Golden Years*, 64-66.

49. Wilder, "Pioneer Girl," 131.

50. Ibid., 140.

51. Wilder, *Little Town on the Prairie*, 28.

52. Ibid., 93-94.

53. Wilder, "Pioneer Girl", 144.

54. Ibid., 133-34.

55. Wilder, *Little House on the Prairie*, 211-12.

56. Ibid., 280, 291-95.

57. Almanzo Wilder to Rose Wilder Lane, questionnaire, Rose Wilder Lane Papers, Manuscripts, Resource Material, *Free Land.*

58. Almanzo Wilder apparently inherited $500 from his parents. James and Angeline Wilder visited Laura and Almanzo in Mansfield in summer 1898, on their way to Louisiana, where the elder Wilders moved at their daughter Eliza Jane's urging. While in Mansfield, James Wilder bought the small house Almanzo and Laura were renting in Mansfield. He gave the house to his son, who later sold it for $500. Rose Wilder Lane later claimed that her grandfather gave her father $500 before he died; at the same time she claimed that James Wilder had lost a fortune of almost $100,000 due to poor investments in Louisiana. William Anderson's research into the Wilder family suggests that her memory was faulty on these points, and that the $500 was an inheritance. James Wilder died in 1899; Angeline in 1905. See Anderson, *Laura Ingalls Wilder*, 164-65; Holtz, *Ghost in the Little House*, 41-42; n. 27, 391.

59. Whose hunger and whose feelings are reflected in the texts remain an important question. Certainly both Rose Wilder Lane and Laura Ingalls Wilder experienced childhood poverty; both carried some anger. Of her mother's habit of writing her manuscripts in pencil, filling lined "Fifty-Fifty" school tablets that cost a nickel apiece, Rose once commented, "That's the Scotch, plus the hungry pioneer; she doesn't waste an inch of the cheapest paper." Anderson, *Laura Wilder of Mansfield*, 14. This is not to suggest that the warmth and security of the novels should be discounted, but that we should interpret carefully, mindful of their joint production, of filters of memory and nostalgia, and of the realities of pioneer poverty and how children might have experienced it. On pioneer childhood, see Elliott West, *Growing Up With the Country* (Albuquerque: University of New Mexico Press, 1989) and Elizabeth Hampsten, *Settlers' Children* (Norman: University of Oklahoma Press, 1991).

Laura Ingalls Wilder:
An Elementary School
Teacher's Perspective

ANN WELLER DAHL

For some years now I have studied, written, taught, and lectured about Laura Ingalls Wilder and her classics for children collectively known as the Little House books. During this period I have become increasingly fascinated with the entire body of Wilder's writing. Of particular interest to me have been the reasons why Mrs. Wilder penned the children's series, why the books instantly became and have remained so popular, the literary devices she employed, and especially the wholesome philosophy of life reflected in these classics.

Many people with whom I share my enthusiasm about Wilder's novels are surprised to learn that the author was sixty-five years old when the first Little House book was published in 1932. Because they know so little about her life they falsely assume that Laura was a "late bloomer."

That was not the case at all. By the time she had published the first of her Little House books, Wilder had been writing articles for a farm journal, the *Missouri Ruralist*, and several other publications for more than twenty years. And prior to her magazine career, she mastered the art of story telling by becoming the "eyes" for her blind older sister, Mary. And before *that*, she and her siblings learned from the tales her father told on those cold winter nights on the prairie.

Also of note was the fact that Wilder was encouraged by her daughter Rose Wilder Lane, to become a professional writer. During the 1920s, long before her mother's name was recognized beyond regional audiences, Lane was well known as a journalist and writer. Indeed, it was Lane who was largely responsible for her mother's entry into the world of children's literature.

It is important, to examine Wilder's writing style and philosophy as well as the details of the Little House books. I will focus first on the Little House books themselves, delving into the reasons they were written and why they have remained popular for so long. Next, I will examine the various literary devices employed by the author to create exciting, coordinated stories, and finally I'll consider examples of the lasting, wholesome philosophy of life reflected in the series.

Let me first address a persistent question: Why in the world would a woman in her early sixties take on the rigors of writing children's literature? After all, Wilder had already ended her career as a writer and household editor for the *Missouri Ruralist*. She also had given up her duties as secretary-treasurer of her local farm loan association. In fact, Wilder and her husband Almanzo had greatly reduced their activities around Rocky Ridge Farm by the late 1920s and had sold a portion of the nearly two hundred acres of their land near Mansfield, Missouri—all of this prior to beginning her career as a children's author.

There are a number of reasons why Wilder returned to the writing desk—one which was personal; a second was practical; and the third reason might be described as emotional. Wilder articulated the personal reason for writing the Little House books in a speech to the Sorosis Club in nearby Mountain Grove, Missouri: "For years I had thought that the stories my father once told me should be passed on to other children. I felt they were much too good to be lost."[1] She did, in fact, write what she thought would be her book (singular) of family history and treasured stories in memory of her beloved father.

Several years later at a book fair in Detroit in 1937, Wilder expanded on this reason for recording her family's story: "I began to think what a wonderful childhood I had had. How I had seen the whole frontier, the woods, the Indian country of the great plains, the frontier towns, the building of the railroads in the wild, unsettled country, homesteading, and farmers coming in to take possession. Then I understood that in my own life I represented a whole period of American history.... I wanted children now to understand more about the beginnings of things, to know what is behind the things they see—what it is that made America as they know it. Then I thought of writing the story of my childhood...an eight volume historical novel covering every aspect of the American frontier."[2]

Another reason was not personal—it was clearly practical. Even with her compensation from the *Missouri Ruralist* and other publications, Wilder had often struggled financially. Lane, now famous and commanding thousands of dollars for her novels and serialized stories in such magazines as the *Saturday Evening Post* and *Country Gentleman*, saw book writing as a way to increase her parents' income. Lane would assist her mother with the typing and editing, and she knew how to work with agents and publishers.

In contrast to the first two reasons, Wilder's third reason was not practical at all, and went beyond the personal toward the emotional. Lane and her mother envisioned such a book as a way to express the very strong feelings they had in favor of individual perseverance in the face of adversity and in opposition to governmental assistance programs. The idea of receiving help from the government did not sit well with either Wilder or Lane. Readers of the Little House books soon discover that an admiration for a spirit of independence runs through the stories. Wilder herself stated as much at the previously noted Sorosis club meeting: "In the Depression following the Civil War, my parents lost all their savings in a bank failure. When possible, they turned the bad into good. If not possible, they endured it. Neither they nor their neighbors begged for help. No other person, nor the government, owed them a living. They owed that to themselves and in some way they paid the debt. And they found their own way."[3] During the 1930s in this country, that message of courage and independence against all odds must have given hope to everyone who heard Wilder's speeches and read the Little House series.

Wilder first penned a book titled "Pioneer Girl" written in true autobiographical style, but neither that book nor its much shorter successor, a story called "When Grandma Was a Little Girl," appealed to the magazine editors who, Lane had hoped, would publish it in serial form. "Ironically," notes biographer, John Miller, "had the *Saturday Evening Post* or some other publisher been willing to take the autobiography at this time, she probably would have become a one-shot nonfiction wonder and Laura Ingalls Wilder—the beloved children's author—probably never would have been discovered."[4]

What finally did appeal to a publisher was yet another version of the manuscript, written not in the first but in the third person, the book that today we know as *Little House in the Big Woods*, which came about in this way. Marion Fiery of Alfred A. Knopf's juvenile department liked the "Grandma" manuscript, but suggested that Wilder lengthen the stories considerably, add details about everyday things of the period, and rewrite the stories for readers from about age eight to age twelve.

It was good advice but Knopf never published the book. Because of financial pressures related to the Depression, Knopf was forced to close its children's department, and the final version of Wilder's family story was actually published by Harper and Brothers and the rest, as they say, is history. That one book eventually became a carefully planned series of seven books about her family and one about her husband's boyhood in upper New York State. These were published between 1932 and 1943. A ninth book, which we know as *The First Four Years*, was found in Wilder's papers after her death, and was not published until 1971, three years after Lane's death.

What made the Little House books instantly popular and to remain so to this day? What made children and their parents love the books so much that they urged Wilder to write more and more? There are several reasons:

First, I believe that most readers enjoy the fact that the characters in the books are *real* people who lived in *real* places and that one of the characters was, indeed, the author of the books. The characters appear in book after book, so readers come to know them well, seeing them mature as they themselves mature and watch them have experiences similar, if not identical, to their own. A curiosity develops as to what will happen next to these "friends" on the prairie, and a real loss is felt when the series ends.

Ann Romines, author of *Constructing the Little House: Gender, Culture, and Laura Ingalls Wilder*, tells most poignantly of how crushed she was as a child when, on the last page of the *These Happy Golden Years*, she came to those so-very-final words: "The End of the Little House Books." Romines concludes her own book with this comment: "Perhaps I have written this book...to postpone, for at least another chapter, 'The End of the Little House Books.'"[5] Thousands of children over the years have no doubt reacted in the same way when they realized that "Laura Ingalls Wilder" would not be telling them another story.

Second, Wilder described people, places, and things so well that readers feel as though they are right there with the characters. The author was skilled at introducing a variety of literary devices that made her words come alive, and her many books tie neatly together into a well-coordinated, multi-volume historical novel. More will be said about this shortly.

Third, these books become longer and increasingly more complex, thereby challenging readers as they grow in their reading skills and as the books' characters grow older. Thus the eight year old child can easily read about and understand what the eight year old Laura is doing, while the eleven year old child can appreciate the way Wilder discussed her late childhood and early adolescent years.

Fourth, the books quite painlessly "teach" geography, pioneer history, and the culture of late nineteenth century America. They delve into many aspects of the natural world of that time. So carefully are certain things described that the children often can imitate the activity or visualize the natural event.

Fifth, the wholesome values upheld in these stories frequently serve as teaching tools that are utilized by parents because often they echo the values already respected in the homes of the children reading the books. As Anita Clair Fellman has noted, "the values and relationships described in Wilder's stories have served as benchmarks against which Americans have measured their own families."[6]

Sixth, the series provides ample opportunities for individual reflection as well as family or classroom discussion. Looking just at *Little House in the Big Woods*, readers and their families, or a class might ponder Cousin Charley's trick of "crying wolf" or the parental instruction that children must share their favorite playthings. They might recall stories that are special only to *their* families (as Pa told stories unique to the Ingalls family) or list things, often inexpensive items that the pioneers had to make or buy at great expense but which today are common. Sometimes the rules laid down by Ma and Pa Ingalls seem very different from ours and often harsh to children today. Were Ma and Pa always right in doing what they did? How might we handle similar situations today?

Finally, I must acknowledge that the popular television show of the 1970s and early 1980s, based much-too-loosely on the Little House books, also contributed to unabated popularity of the Wilder series. Although the shows frequently strayed far from the original stories, they nonetheless did retain the most important theme that runs from the beginning to the end of the classics: the love and strength of the family unit. Incidentally, the very fact that the television shows were so different from the books makes for good classroom discussion. Were the plots similar, silly, reasonable, and so forth? Where were the major differences between the books and the television shows?

These seven reasons all combine to make the Little House books particularly suited for use as a read-aloud, family activity. Not only are they enjoyed today by nuclear families, they are also used for inter-generational sharing between grandparents and grandchildren, and by groups of home schooling families who meet regularly to discuss them.

There are additional, more subtle qualities that make these books so popular. Let us now examine more closely some of those literary devices that Wilder employed in her writing, making the books instantly appealing to the readers of the 1930s and 1940s as well as those today.

First, I must mention again the author's superb descriptions of people, places, and things. These are presented in vivid pictures or clear, orderly detail. On the opening page of *The Long Winter*, for example, Wilder uses expressive language that quickly engages readers: "The sky was high and quivering with heat over the shimmering prairie. Halfway down to sunset the sun blazed as hotly as at noon." In the same chapter, "...the muskrats woke and went pattering down the smooth mud-floor of their hallway. They plunged into the black water and came up through the pool to the wide, wild night under the sky."[7] Not only do children love these descriptions, they imitate them in their own compositions.

Second, Wilder employed figures of speech to make associations that her readers could understand. Among these were the familiar figures like simile and metaphor, hyperbole, and a great deal of personification. She also introduced less familiar ones like synecdoche, when a part of something represents the whole. This figure is most familiar to us in the idea of a groom asking for a bride's hand in marriage. Surely he wants more than just her hand! Wilder uses this device several times in the books, e.g., in *Little House on the Prairie*; Laura's foot is being "naughty."

Third, the books offer frequent opportunities for vocabulary development. Children may simply learn the meaning of new words, like pessimist/optimist or herbivore/carnivore or nocturnal/diurnal, or they may delve into their root meanings from other languages. Students are also exposed to familiar idioms and time-worn sayings: Make hay while the sun shines...Putting up false fronts...All's well that ends well...Where there's a will there's a way.

Fourth, Wilder effectively uses contrasts and comparisons. The sweat worked up by Laura and her Pa as they "make hay while the sun shines" is a far cry from the shivers they experience while huddled by the inadequate stove in the book titled *The Long Winter*. The always-plentiful supply of pancakes at the Wilder boys' bachelor quarters is a stark contrast to the conditions of near-starvation at the Ingalls' home. Divisions between a man's work and a woman's work are strictly drawn, but of necessity, the line is sometimes crossed. Ma Ingalls fears Indians while Pa Ingalls is quite tolerant of them. There is safety and security in the home while outside is wilderness and danger. Chapters of "comic" or perhaps "pleasant" relief separate serious sections of the books.

Fifth, Wilder sometimes utilized devices that make the reader particularly anxious to know what will come next. Students are encouraged to look for the "little surprise" that brightens up the day, or the "little mystery" that encourages the reader to push on until the mysterious situation is resolved. An excellent example of the "little surprise" occurs in *The Long Winter* when Ma and the girls secretly concoct an "apple" pie out of green pumpkin, then excitedly wait all day for Pa to return home to eat it!

Sometimes the "little mysteries" are quickly solved. In the same story, Laura is puzzled by a sound she is hearing, and after only four or five lines, the solution comes: Laura is hearing the "silence" that follows the howl of a blizzard. Much later in the story, a much longer, more dramatic mystery keeps readers rapidly turning pages. Will Almanzo and Cap find the settler rumored to have wheat? If so, will they be able to buy the wheat, then return safely to DeSmet? So artfully written is this portion of *The Long Winter* that Wilder even changed the subject in a "meanwhile back at the ranch" manner, in the middle of the search story. This forces the reader to wait through an entire chapter, unrelated to the search story, before discovering whether or not the boys return safely and with wheat.

Sixth, within the stories, the plot lines usually have important sub-divisions or mini-climaxes. Think of *On the Banks of Plum Creek* where readers finally discover what grasshopper weather is, wait for the grasshoppers to disappear, and wonder whether or not Pa will ever be able to grow a successful wheat crop or will be forced to move the family again. In a similar vein, consider the four distinct subdivisions in *The Long Winter*, the confirmation by the Indian that the winter would be long and hard, the announcement that the train would not come until the spring thaw, the purchase of the wheat by the two boys and their safe return to town, and the happy statement that the train has finally arrived bringing the much-needed supplies.

Earlier we discussed the fact that children have always liked the use of continuing characters in the Little House books. There is another device employed by Wilder that also provides a sense of continuity. I refer to the use of repeated themes. From my experience, highlighting these themes, both in my Baltimore classroom and through my work with Calvert home schoolers around the world, I can say that the "game" of "spot the theme" is not only meaningful, but also fun for children who quickly become skilled at it.

The themes come in three varieties: those of a general nature that run throughout the entire series or a large segment of the series, those belonging to individual books, and those associated with particular characters.

Many of the general themes may be classified as "values" found in Wilder's philosophy of life as seen in the Little House books. In addition to those values—themes, the reader can follow throughout the series such themes as Pa's constant desire to move farther and farther West and Ma's equally strong desire to stay in areas having a church and a school for her family. Evident from book one to eight is the presence of self-generated entertainment that constantly lifts the family's spirits and enriches their days. Readers will also find among the many themes one dealing with the changing role of the woman on the frontier.

A second group of themes is associated with the individual books. In *On the Banks of Plum Creek*, Pa makes it quite clear that he wants to grow the perfect wheat crop so his family may have the finer things of life. Establishing the central plot line (what Lane termed the pattern and I am calling the book's theme) of *The Long Winter* was, as John Miller points out, a difficult task for Wilder. Writing to her daughter about her plot-line dilemma the author remarked, "There seems to be nothing to it, only the struggle to live, through the winter, until spring comes again." As Miller comments, "In the end, she realized that the struggle against the elements was the obvious, and compelling, central theme for the book."[8] Readers who have "suffered" with the Ingalls through those horrid eight months of 1880-81 will realize that the story is, indeed, simply one of survival.

As the series progresses, it becomes obvious that certain characteristics may be associated with each of the Ingalls family members. (Here, the word "characteristic" is more appropriate to use than "theme.") Laura is a person with a deep appreciation for nature and identification with it. She fears strangers and towns, though she generally has an adventuresome spirit. Mary is basically the opposite of Laura: she tends to accept things as they are, loves home-centered activities, and is seen as perfect by Laura. Pa adores sharing his fiddle and his stories with the family, and Ma prides herself on keeping a refined home.

Usually we don't think of a child's book as a type of literature that reflects a personal philosophy of life. But Wilder's various beliefs are clearly reflected in her writings, and you may logically surmise that *her* children's books *do indeed* reflect a number of such philosophies. Foremost among them, of course, must be her emphasis on the strength of the family unit, followed closely by a respect for religion, education, nature, cooperation, and the simple things of life. After reading the Little House books, I think you will agree that many, if not all of Wilder's principles are worth applying to your life today and in the future, just as Wilder realized that they were an important part of her life growing up one hundred-twenty-plus years ago.

Perhaps Wilder's own words best explain the lasting appeal and values of her books. "The Little House books are stories of long ago. The way we live and your schools are much different now. So many changes have made living and learning easier. *But the real things haven't changed* [italics added]. It is still best to be honest and truthful; to make the most of what we have; to be happy with simple pleasures, and to be cheerful and have courage when things go wrong."[9] These comments come from a composite letter prepared by Wilder in 1947 for children who wrote to her about her books. Although her words are more than fifty years old, and the world she wrote about is more than a century old, her books have remained popular and relevant even to the present day for, as Wilder said, "...the real things haven't changed."[10]

Endnotes

1. *Little House Sampler*, William T. Anderson, ed., (Lincoln, University of Nebraska Press, 1988): 176-77

2. Ibid., 217

3. Ibid., 180

4. John E. Miller, *Becoming Laura Ingalls Wilder: The Woman Behind the Legend* (Columbia, University of Missouri Press, 1998), 183.

5. Ann Romines, *Constructing the Little House: Gender, Culture, and Laura Ingalls Wilder* (Amherst, University of Massachusetts Press, 1988), 256.

6. Anita Clair Fellman, "Laura Ingalls Wilder and Rose Wilder Lane: The Politics of a Mother-Daughter Relationship," *Signs: Journal of Women in Culture and Society* 15 (1990): 535-561.

7. Wilder, *The Long Winter* (New York, Harper & Row, 1940, 1953), 1, 11.

8. Miller, *Becoming Laura Ingalls Wilder*, 235.

9. Wilder, Composite Letter to Children, February 1947, Laura Ingalls Wilder file, State Historical Society of Missouri.

10. Ibid.

Afterword

I would like to again thank the contributors for the essays found in this volume. They have made significant contributions to our understanding of Laura Ingalls Wilder's impact on the study of the history of the American West, its exploration, socialization, and influence on social values.

I would also like to thank Cindy Worrell for her many efforts in typing this manuscript and Janlyn Ewald for designing the volume. A major debt of gratitude is owed to Timothy Walch for his guidance in the editing and formatting process. His advice has been invaluable. Any errors, omissions, or other shortcomings are the responsibility of the editor.

As a coda to this volume I would like to respond to the frequently asked question, "Why are the Laura Ingalls Wilder papers a part of the historical collections of the Herbert Hoover Presidential Library?" In 1978, William T. Anderson came to the Library to conduct research on Rose Wilder Lane and Herbert Hoover, a relationship that began with her book, *The Making of Herbert Hoover*, which was published as a campaign biography in 1920. After completing his research, Anderson, who was aware that Roger Lea MacBride, heir to the Lane/Wilder papers, was seeking an appropriate repository, inquired if the Library would be interested in adding the Lane papers to its holdings. Considering their early association and her subsequent friendship with Hoover that continued until his death in 1964, it was determined that it was a collection that fell within the Library's range of interest. Anderson then put the Library in contact with MacBride.

As the senior archivist at that time, it was my responsibility to visit MacBride and, after several trips to Charlottesville, Virginia, he chose the Hoover Library to house the collection. I later learned that this decision was based on several factors: aside from our obvious interest in acquiring the collection, he had been informed by Anderson that the Hoover Library facilities offered state of the art preservation and security; and that our finding aids made it possible to access collections with a minimum amount of time and a maximum degree of accuracy. Also of importance was that this facility is centrally located between the Mansfield, Missouri and DeSmet, South Dakota which were, and remain, the locus of ongoing research on the life of Rose Wilder Lane and Laura Ingalls Wilder.

When Roger MacBride notified us in 1980 that we were to have the papers, I returned to Charlottesville to transport them to Washington, DC for transshipment to West Branch. It was then that MacBride casually asked if the Library also wanted her mother's papers. This was the first mention in this negotiation of the existence and availability of the Laura Ingalls Wilder papers. A cursory examination revealed that the two collections were so interwoven that it would have been a gross disservice to scholars to separate them. As a result, both were accepted and the Laura Ingalls Wilder files now form a series within the Rose Wilder Lane papers.

Not all of the Rose Wilder Lane/Laura Ingalls Wilder papers came from MacBride's holdings in Charlottesville. Early in 1982, I began making arrangements with MacBride to pay a visit to the Laura Ingalls Wilder Home and Museum in Mansfield, Missouri. He had informed me that portions of the Lane/Wilder papers were in storage upstairs in the home and that he wished to donate those materials to the Hoover Library.

After several months of discussion, we reached a mutually agreeable date. I drove to Springfield, picked him up at the airport, and together we went over to Mansfield where I then had the pleasure of meeting Irene Lichty LeCount who toured us through the Wilder Museum and Home. At that time, only the first floor of the home was open to public viewing. LeCount expressed her concerns regarding the preservation of memorabilia, particularly in the home. This opened a friendly relationship between the Library and the Wilder Museum and Home as we discussed measures that could be taken to preserve this vital part of the Wilder heritage.

We then went upstairs to review various materials that MacBride wished me to consider for inclusion in the Lane/Wilder papers in West Branch. A room by room search introduced me to that part of the home described by Rose in her correspondence and journal entries. There was the sleeping porch in an unrestored state appearing not unlike a photograph found in the Lane/Wilder papers. There also were bedrooms containing furniture, closets with miscellaneous articles of clothing and many unmarked boxes everywhere.

For an archivist, the excitement surrounding an unexplored closet or an unopened box remains perpetually stimulating, and this particular search was not disappointing. The remarkable collection found there included correspondence, book manuscripts, and photographs. While not extensive in quantity, the reference value is difficult to overestimate. Contained in this accretion were typescripts, with handwritten changes by both Wilder and Lane, of *Little House on the Prairie, On the Banks of Plum Creek, By the Shores of Silver Lake, The Long Winter,* and *Little Town on the Prairie.* Also a part of this accretion were articles, newspaper clippings, postcards, a selection of Wilder's letters from children, and photographs of Lane and the Wilder family, and of Lane's travels in Europe, the Mid-East, Armenia, Albania, and Greece. Although this cache amounted to only 2 ½ linear feet of textual documentation, it contained material central to biographical works on both Wilder and Lane and to critical studies of their writings.

MacBride continued to locate and forward materials to the Library including important items such as Wilder's handwritten draft of *The First Four Years* along with isolated draft materials, photographs, and other files. These gifts continued through April 1984 bringing the Lane/Wilder collection to a total of 30 linear feet of which 3 linear feet comprise the Laura Ingalls Wilder series. MacBride maintained an unabated interest in both the Library's programs and the development and use of the Lane/Wilder papers. His death in March 1995 was a tragic loss of a personal friend of the Hoover Library and myself.

It is difficult to estimate the significance of this gift to the Hoover Presidential Library. As the most heavily used collection in the Library's holdings after the papers of Herbert Hoover, it is the foundation for scholarly biographies of both Rose Wilder Lane and Laura Ingalls Wilder. These papers provided the impetus for a major conference and scholarly papers found in this and other publications, along with a 1995 winter exhibit in the museum that drew the largest number of visitors for any show mounted by the Hoover Library during that season of the year.

Of greater significance is that access to these historical materials has provided an appreciation of the contributions of Laura Ingalls Wilder in a multiplicity of roles that are unfolding in the writings of today's scholars. Initially appreciated as a premier author of children books, she is now being viewed from the perspective of women's studies and as a chronicler of history of the American frontier. This legacy is one that the Herbert Hoover Presidential Library is privileged to preserve and make available to a host of admirers in both scholarly and lay communities.

Dwight M. Miller
Iowa City, Iowa

Contributors

John E. Miller, Professor of History at the University of South Dakota, has published a substantial number of articles and book length works on Laura Ingalls Wilder. These include, "Place and Community in the Little Town on the Prairie," *South Dakota History*; "Freedom and Control in Laura Ingalls Wilder's De Smet," *Great Plains Quarterly*; *Laura Ingalls Wilder's Little Town: Where History and Literature Meet*, University Press of Kansas; and most recently, *Becoming Laura Ingalls Wilder: A Biography*, University of Missouri Press.

Ann Romines is Director of the Graduate Program and Professor of English at The George Washington University. She is the author of *The Home Plot: Women, Writing and Domestic Ritual*, University of Massachusetts Press; *Constructing the Little House: Gender, Culture, and Laura Ingalls Wilder*, University of Massachusetts Press, which received the 1999 Children's Literature Association Award, and many essays on American women's writing and culture. She is also editor of *Willa Cather's Southern Connections: New Essays on Cather and the South*, University Press of Virginia.

Anita Clair Fellman is Director of the Women's Studies Program at Old Dominion University. Her most recent book, co-edited with Veronica Strong-Boag, is the third edition of *Rethinking Canada: The Promise of Women's History*, Oxford University Press. She is the author of numerous articles on Wilder and on the Little House books and is completing a book on the place of the Little House books in American culture.

Elizabeth Jameson holds the Imperial Oil & Lincoln McKay Chair of American Studies at the University of Calgary. Her publications include: *All That Glitters: Class, Conflict, and Community in Cripple Creek; The Women's West* and *Writing the Range: Race, Class, and Culture in the Women's West* (both with Susan Armitage); and "In Search of the Great Ma," *Journal of the West* (April 1998). She is researching Laura Ingalls Wilder's and Rose Wilder Lane's narratives of the pioneer experience for a book on gender and western history.

Ann Weller Dahl has taught for twenty-nine years at the Calvert School in Baltimore, Maryland. As part of her fourth grade curriculum she has presented annually a unit on Laura Ingalls Wilder and her Little House books. Dahl's interest in this subject led her to apply for and receive several times, the School's Garrett Summer Study Grant. These awards have enabled her to visit all the Little House sites twice and to study this subject in depth. This resulted in her writing detailed reading guides for the Little House books for use by the home schooling division of the Calvert School.

Suggestions for Further Reading and Research

When Laura Ingalls Wilder set pencil to paper writing "Pioneer Girl", little did she know that twenty five years later, millions of copies of her books would be sold around the world. Not surprisingly, this body of work has attracted the attention of an international group of scholars who have examined Wilder's life, the events described in her writings, the relationship between Wilder, her husband Almanzo and their daughter Rose Wilder Lane, and the influence of Lane on her mother's writings. The following described materials and publications will assist readers in attaining a greater knowledge and understanding of these individuals and the events surrounding them.

Primary Sources

The most important place to begin research on Laura Ingalls Wilder is her papers which form a series within the Rose Wilder Lane papers found in the archival holdings of the Herbert Hoover Presidential Library. Amounting to three linear feet of correspondence with her daughter Rose Wilder Lane and other family members, drafts of books and other writings, drawings, and related historical materials, these papers are an invaluable source of documentation on interpersonal relationships, historical events, and the writing of the Little House books. The Lane papers contain additional correspondence files and detailed diaries and notes that offer further insight into the mother/daughter relationship and the writing of the Little House books.

The Hoover Library also holds the holograph draft of the *The First Four Years*, and typescripts of the "Pioneer Girl" manuscript versions sent to literary agents Carl Brandt and George T. Bye, and typescript drafts of *Farmer Boy, Little House on the Prairie, On the Banks of Plum Creek, By the Shores of Silver Lake, The Long Winter, Little Town on the Prairie,* and *These Happy Golden Years.* Many of these drafts contain handwritten changes by both Wilder and Lane. The handwritten drafts of *The Long Winter* and *These Happy Golden Years* are in the Detroit Public Library, and *The Little Town on the Prairie* draft was given to the Pomona, California Public Library. The balance of the penciled drafts of the Little House books, and "Pioneer Girl" are part of the historical holdings of the Laura Ingalls Wilder Home and Museum at Mansfield, Missouri. A microfilm publication of the The Wilder Home and Museum manuscript holdings entitled, *Laura Ingalls Wilder Papers, 1894-1943,* is available from the University of Missouri Western Historical Manuscript Collection, Columbia, Missouri. A copy of this publication is also available for research in the Hoover Library reading room.

Another valuable resource for the study of Laura Ingalls Wilder found in the Hoover Presidential Library archives is the research collection assembled by William Holtz in the course of writing *Ghost in the Little House.* Although this work is a biography of Rose Wilder Lane, it contains a substantial amount of material pertaining to Laura Ingalls Wilder and the writing of the Little House books. Any serious student should plan to spend time with this collection in addition to the Lane/Wilder papers.

Secondary Sources

There is a wealth of published materials about Laura Ingalls Wilder that offer both the serious researcher and the casual reader information on, and insight into, the life and works of Laura Ingalls Wilder. Several biographical studies for both adult and young readers provide analytical overviews of this subject in addition to a host of articles and monographs including the following selection of publications:

Anderson, William T. *Laura Ingalls Wilder: A Biography,* New York, HarperCollins, 1992. This young reader biography covering Wilder's childhood, family travels, and adult years in Mansfield, Missouri, provides a good introduction to the study of Wilder's life and events.

_____. *Laura Ingalls Wilder: The Iowa Story.* Burr Oak, Iowa, Laura Ingalls Wilder Park and Museum, 1990. This booklet describing the two-year period of the Ingalls travels not accounted for in the Little House series provides useful information for both the serious and casual reader.

_____. "The Literary Apprenticeship of Laura Ingalls Wilder." Vol. 13 (Winter, 1983); and, "Laura Ingalls Wilder and Rose Wilder Lane: The Continuing Collaboration," Vol. 16 (Summer, 1986) *South Dakota History*. These two articles are among the most worthwhile and most frequently cited works on the subject of the writings of Laura Ingalls Wilder and the contributions of Rose Wilder Lane. Anderson also discusses Wilder's early efforts as a journalist and how they prepared her for more ambitious projects.

_____. *A Little House Sampler.* New York, Harper & Row, 1988. This compilation further discusses the writing relationship between Wilder and her daughter Rose. It also includes some of the earliest examples of Wilder's writings, much of it autobiographical in nature, and is of substantial value to students of both Wilder and Lane.

Fellman, Anita, Clair. "Laura Ingalls Wilder and Rose Wilder Lane: The Politics of a Mother-Daughter Relationship," *Signs,* Spring, 1990. This well researched and often cited article explores and analyzes both the personal relationship between mother and daughter and how their political philosophy was expressed in their writings.

Fraser, Caroline. "The Prairie Queen." *New York Review of Books* 41, December 22, 1994: 38-45. This author argues in a convincing fashion that although this was a collaborative effort between mother and daughter, Wilder was the author of the Little House books.

Hines, Stephen W., ed. *I Remember Laura: Laura Ingalls Wilder.* Nashville, Thomas Nelson, Inc., 1994. A compilation of Wilder's early writings along with edited materials. The primary value of this work is a collection of interviews with people who knew the Wilders.

_____. *Little House in the Ozarks: A Laura Ingalls Wilder Sampler, The Rediscovered Writings,* Nashville, Thomas Nelson, Inc., 1991. Primarily a compilation of Wilder articles reprinted from *The Missouri Ruralist.* A lack of citations however, greatly hampers it as a useful reference tool.

The Horn Book's Laura Ingalls Wilder: Articles About and By Laura Ingalls Wilder, Garth Williams, and the Little House Books. William T.

Anderson, ed. Davison, Michigan, Anderson Publications, 1987. This booklet reprinted from the September 1943 and December 1953 *Horn Book* issues include classic articles by Virginia Kirkus, Ann Carrol Moore, Garth Williams, Marcia Dalphin, Irene Smith, and an introduction by the editor.

Holtz, William. *The Ghost in the Little House: A Life of Rose Wilder Lane.* Columbia, London, University of Missouri Press, 1993. Although this is a biography of Rose Wilder Lane, Holtz explores her relationship with her mother, Laura Ingalls Wilder, and the writing of the Little House books in depth and detail. Holtz concludes that even though the portrayal of events and characters found in the writings are the work of Wilder, they were rewritten, and in large part, ghosted by Lane. These assertions have been warmly contested by other scholars including contributors to this volume.

_____. "Closing the Circle: The American Optimism of Laura Ingalls Wilder." *Great Plains Quarterly* 4, 1984, 79-90. This article is a discussion of the Little House books in terms of their social, political and religious contexts. Holtz also states that the pain and distress of the pioneer experience was so great that it prevented the publication of *The First Four Years* during Wilder's lifetime.

Laura Ingalls Wilder Lore. Laura Ingalls Wilder Memorial Society, De Smet, South Dakota. First published in 1975, this semi-annual newsletter covers current events at De Smet and other Wilder sites along with articles about Laura Ingalls Wilder and Rose Wilder Lane, book reviews, obituaries, interviews, reminiscences of pioneer times and other useful information.

Miller, John E. *Laura Ingalls Wilder's Little Town: Where History and Literature Meet.* Lawrence, Kansas, University Press of Kansas, 1994. This well researched and useful study brings the reader into contact with both "history lived" (as portrayed in the Little House books) and the synthesis found in history textbooks. The author finds them complementary in providing a realistic portrait of the pioneer west.

_____. *Becoming Laura Ingalls Wilder: The Woman Behind the Legend*, Columbia and London, University of Missouri Press, 1998. This biographical study concentrates on Wilder's life after she moves to Mansfield, Missouri and how her life is reflected in her writings. He also describes in depth and detail the writing of the Little House books and the collaboration between Wilder and her daughter, Rose Wilder Lane. This is the definitive biography of Wilder.

Mooney-Getoff, Mary J. *Laura Ingalls Wilder: A Bibliography.* Southold, New York, Wise Owl Press, 1980. This compilation of titles of books, articles, and audio-visual resources through 1979, includes biography, literary criticism, and several other categories. Even though it is quite dated, it contains entries that are of continuing interest and value to researchers.

Moore, Rosa Ann. "Laura Ingalls Wilder and Rose Wilder Lane: The Chemistry of Collaboration." *Children's Literature in Education* 11 (Autumn, 1980): 101-109. This author had access to the Lane/Wilder papers prior to their deposit in the Herbert Hoover Presidential Library enabling her to publish documented literary criticism in advance of other scholars. She determined that even though Lane contributed to the stories, it was Wilder who imbued them with the qualities most highly valued by her readers.

_____. "Laura Ingalls Wilder's Orange Notebooks and the Art of the Little House Books." *Childrens Literature* 4 (1975): 105-19. Moore was one of the first literary critics to publish that Wilder did not emerge as a fully blossomed author at the age of 65 without considerable effort. This article explores and analyzes changes in order and dimension between *The First Four Years* and *These Happy Golden Years.*

_____. "The Little House Books: Rose-Colored Classics," *Childrens Literature* 7 (1978): 7-16. This analysis of correspondence between Wilder and Lane concerns the apprenticeship of Wilder as an author, and the subsequent collaboration of the writing of the Little House books. In this article, Moore argues that Wilder, not Lane, generated the books.

Romines, Ann. *Constructing the Little House: Gender, Culture and Laura Ingalls Wilder.* Amherst, Massachusetts, University of Massachusetts Press, 1997. Written from a feminist perspective, the author examines each of the Little House Books, and the gender elements of frontier homes. She also analyzes the mother/daughter relationship and their collaboration in writing the series. It is the best book length feminist treatment of these subjects.

_____. "Writing the 'Little House': The Architecture of a Series." *Great Plains Quarterly* 14 (Spring 1994): 107-115. This article which predates the above entry, shares much of the same material but remains useful for details.

Spaeth, Janet. *Laura Ingalls Wilder.* Boston, Twayne Publishers, 1987. A component of the Twayne author's series, this work examines the Little House books from biographical, historical and sociological perspectives.

Subramanian, Jane M. *Laura Ingalls Wilder: An Annotated Bibliography of Critical, Biographical and Teaching Studies.* Westport, Connecticut, Greenwood Press, 1997. This bibliography is divided into the following subject areas: critical commentary, biographical works, teaching studies, teaching kits, serial publications, and book reviews of the Little House books at the time of their publication. This is the most comprehensive, published Wilder bibliography available.

Zochert, Donald. *The Life of Laura Ingalls Wilder.* Chicago: Henry Regenery, 1976. This biography focuses on Wilder's early life with each chapter devoted to a different geographical locale. It includes descriptions of Wilder friends and family and brief accounts of her adulthood and career as an author. This work which contains much useful information for both lay and academic readers, is based largely on "Pioneer Girl."

INDEX

15, 49, 74, 78, 97
and violence, 84
and western movement, 73, 84
Pioneer journeys, 4
"Politics of a Mother-Daughter
Relationship," 23
Populist Party, 76
"Prairie Home Companion," 45

Reagan, Ronald, and individualism,
47-48
Rocky Ridge Farm, 81
Romines, Ann,
feminist interpretation of LH
books, 5, 6, 21, 49, 64
mention of, 1, 4, 6, 50, 98
Roosevelt, Theodore, 76
Rosenzweig, Linda, 23

Saturday Evening Post, 96, 97
Seal, Neta and Silas, 16
"Significance of History, The," 69-73,
76
Spaeth, Janet, 7, 21
Sorosis Club, 96, 97
Spring Valley, Minnesota, 81
Stratemeyer series (*Nancy Drew,
Hardy Boys*), 52

These Happy Golden Years, 2, 4, 14,
30, 74, 78, 84, 98
Tom Sawyer, 31
Trilling, Lionel, 17
Turner, Frederick Jackson,
and feminine role, 86
and pioneer past, 82, 88
mention of, 30, 69-77

U.S. Census, 1890, 75

*University of Chicago Alumni
Magazine*, 45

Vitense, Marjorie, 43

Walch, Timothy, 105
Walker, Barbara M., 60
Walnut Grove, Minnesota, 73-74
Washington Post, 45
"When Grandma Was a Little Girl,"
97
Wilder, Almanzo James
biographical resources, 16
courtship of LIW, 3, 42
disappointments in life, 86-87
and food, 83
marriage to Laura, 13, 14, 23,
73, 78
tree claim, 74
mention of, 18, 29, 36, 46
Wilder, Eliza Jane, 25, 83
Wilder, James 36
Wilder, Laura Ingalls,
as author, 35, 40-42, 43, 45, 49,
60, 73, 95-97
biographic questions, 24
biographic resources, 16
as biographic subject, 13-21
and chautauquas, 61
and closing the frontier, 75
community activities, 20-21
courtship by Almanzo, 3
and Great Depression, 76
Detroit Book Fair speech, 96
employment outside of home, 74,
79
fan mail, 43
food, 83
Indians, attitude toward, 37-38
marital relationship, 23
memorial societies, 58
and Turnerian, narritave, 75-77

in masculine world, 86
papers, 2, 4, 15, 40, 47, 48, 98, 105-107
philosophic values, 101-103
political activities and orientation, 19-20, 24
popularity as novelist, 25, 96
religious activities, 19
role in writing LH books, 2-5, 8, 21-23
school teaching, 84
social life, 20-21

study clubs, 20
vision of American frontier, 1
mention of, 29, 30, 31, 32, 34, 35, 51, 52, 54, 55
Wilkes, Maria, 21
Williams, Garth, 32
Willingham, Terri Lynn, 50-52, 55-56
Wilson, Woodrow, 76
World War II, impact on LH books, 7
Worrell, Cindy, 105
Zochert, Donald, 4, 21

CPSIA information can be obtained at www.ICGtesting.com
Printed in the USA
LVOW111328280212

270806LV00001B/78/P